Glyn Daniel was born and brought up in the Vale of Glamorgan and attended school there until he went up to Cambridge in 1932. Apart from the war, when he served as a Photographic Intelligence Officer in the R.A.F., he has been in Cambridge ever since, as a Fellow of St John's College and a university lecturer in archaeology. In 1971–2 he was George Grant MacCurdy Lecturer in Prehistory at Harvard. Dr Daniel's main interests in archaeology are megalithic monuments, prehistoric art, and the history and method of archaeology. He has written many books, including *The Prehistoric Chamber Tombs of England and Wales* (1950), *A Hundred Years of Archaeology* (1950), *The Megalith Builders of Western Europe* (1958, now in Pelicans), *The Prehistoric Chamber Tombs of France* (1961), and *The Idea of Prehistory* (1962). Since 1957 he has edited the quarterly journal, *Antiquity*, and is general editor of the well-known series, *Ancient Peoples and Places*. For six years he was chairman of the popular B.B.C. features, *Animal, Vegetable, Mineral?* and *Buried Treasure*, and is now a director of Anglia Television and chairman of its programme *What? When? Where?* Widely travelled, Glyn Daniel still prefers France: his discursive guide-book, <u>Lascaux and Carnac</u> (1955), is being reissued in an enlarged edition. Both his detective stories, *The Cambridge Murders* and *Welcome Death*, have appeared in Penguins. His wife shares his archaeological interests and his recreational interests in food, wine and travel.

Get it -

Try to find an old copy of
Layard's *Monuments of Nineveh*
mid 19th C. (1st exc. of Tel. Nineveh)

THE IDEA
OF PREHISTORY

GLYN DANIEL

WITH EIGHT
PLATES

PENGUIN BOOKS

Penguin Books Ltd, Harmondsworth, Middlesex, England
Penguin Books Inc., 7110 Ambassador Road, Baltimore, Maryland 21207, U.S.A.
Penguin Books Australia Ltd, Ringwood, Victoria, Australia

—

First published by C. A. Watts 1962
Published in Pelican Books 1964
Reissued 1971

—

—

Made and printed in Great Britain
by Richard Clay (The Chaucer Press) Ltd,
Bungay, Suffolk
Set in Monotype Bembo

CONTENTS

Acknowledgements are due to the following for the photographs in this book: Plate 1, after *Archaeologia*; Plate 2, by courtesy of Thames & Hudson Photo Archives; Plate 3, Yan; Plate 4 (upper), J. K. St Joseph, University of Cambridge Committee for Aerial Photography, (lower) J. K. St Joseph, Crown copyright reserved; Plate 5 (upper), Crown copyright, (lower) Leisner; Plate 6, National Museum, Copenhagen; Plate 7, National Museum, Prague; Plate 8, Edwin Smith.

PREFACE

WHEN the University of Birmingham honoured me with an invitation to give the Josiah Mason Lectures (founded by the Rationalist Press Association) for the year 1956–7 I thought it might be interesting to devote the eight lectures to a discussion, necessarily brief and sketchy, of the development of the idea of prehistory in Western European and particularly British thought. I had already written a short history of the development of prehistory between 1840 and 1940 in my *Hundred Years of Archaeology*. The Mason lectures seemed to provide a good opportunity for isolating the important events in the history of that hundred years and relating them to what went before and what came after.

These lectures are printed almost exactly as they were given, and are records of the spoken word. I have added to them a few footnotes and some suggestions for further reading, and included eight plates to illustrate various points in the general argument.

It gives me pleasure to record here my thanks to the University for inviting me to give these lectures, and my appreciation of the kindness and hospitality of individual members of that University while I gave them, notably the Vice-Chancellor and the Dean of the Faculty of Arts, Professor Charles Meade, and Professor Sargant Florence.

GLYN DANIEL

St John's College, Cambridge
1 June 1960

CHAPTER ONE

THE FOG AND THE FLOOD

THE first man to use the word prehistory seems to have been Daniel Wilson, and this was just over a hundred years ago, in 1851, in the title of his book *The Archaeology and Prehistoric Annals of Scotland*. In the preface to the second edition of this book published twelve years later Wilson refers to 'the application of the term prehistoric introduced – if I mistake not – for the first time in this work'. To the best of my knowledge Daniel Wilson was not making a mistake and 1851 was the first time that prehistory was introduced into the English language. The *Oxford English Dictionary* records the stages by which the word came into respectable and general usage. Sir Edward Tylor was using it in his *Primitive Culture* in 1871; seven years later Mr Gladstone is using it, and finally it becomes a respectable word – *The Times* mentions prehistory in 1888 and *Nature* follows suit in 1902.

It is not only in England but on the Continent – in France, Switzerland, Germany, the Scandinavian countries, Spain and Italy – that, during the second half of the nineteenth century, prehistory came into existence as a conscious and separate aspect of the study of man's past. The word used was naturally not the same; the French spoke of *préhistoire*, the Italians of *preistoria*, the Germans had the word *Vorgeschichte*, while the Danes had the very nice word *oldtid* – old times. And this is of course what prehistory is concerned with; the old or oldest times in man's past – the very earliest moments in that long story of human development which grows in complexity and historicity from the spread of the Roman Empire to the present day.

In England itself the word prehistory was not immediately

accepted with enthusiasm. Other names were suggested, of which one was <u>antehistory.</u> Sir John Lubbock seriously considered using this word when he was writing the book that was eventually entitled *Prehistoric Times*, and which, published first in 1865, did so much to popularize prehistory. He wisely decided against this word, and, although it was of course spelt with an *e* and not an *i*, it is fortunate that the name was dropped. Others, in the middle of the nineteenth century, and nowadays, have complained that prehistory was a stupid name, because it was essentially a misnomer; it meant, logically and etymologically, the time before history, and surely, it was argued, there was, strictly speaking, no time in the past of man before he had any history. History was essentially human, unless one referred to natural history. What was prehistory, they argued, but the earliest past of history? This is, I suppose, logically correct – not that logic seems to enter very much into nomenclature; names most often grow up and are not carefully thought out.

But it is true that we normally <u>use the word history in two senses,</u> as when we say the <u>history of man,</u> meaning the whole of man's past, and history <u>*sensu stricto*</u>, when we mean the part of man's past which <u>we know about because he has written</u> down details of it – not necessarily always truthfully or correctly – in inscriptions on stones and tombs, in diaries, state papers, treaties, memoirs, and books. In fact by history *sensu stricto* we normally mean in usual parlance written history, and I imagine that most of you still mean written history when you speak of history. Now it is, of course, <u>pre-written history</u> that we <u>mean when we speak of prehistory,</u> and it was the development of the study of man's past before he began to record it himself in symbols that can now be read, that had come to such a stage a hundred years ago that a special word had to be found for it: the word prehistory.

The whole history of man had, of course, been studied long before Daniel Wilson spoke of prehistory. <u>There is, we must</u>

all admit this, a natural, normal, human interest in origins and beginnings. In the world of sixteenth-century German history, the past of man, or universal history, was subdivided according to the four World Empires, i.e. Assyria, Persia, Greece, and Rome – which was to last until the end of the world. This was what is known as the Four-Monarchy System. It was, surprisingly enough, philologists and not historians who introduced the idea of ancient, medieval, and modern history; and this is the division we find in *An Universal History from the Earliest Account of Time* produced in London in thirty-eight volumes between 1736 and 1765. What, then, happened in the mid nineteenth century was that a fourth division was added to the human past, and from then on we have been thinking of history, history in its widest sense, that is – human history – as divided into prehistory, ancient history, medieval history, and modern history. And by the way when I say 'we have been thinking', I am afraid I mean people concerned with ancient history, archaeology, and anthropology. It is true that the general public and our universities are only, rather slowly, getting used to the idea of the antiquity of man and the existence of prehistory. Universities have not necessarily been in the van of intellectual progress. In the first of his Ford Lectures at Oxford in 1907 Professor Haverfield said that the universities – and I think he meant by that phrase at that moment Oxford and Cambridge – had never been interested in archaeology, and that our greatest archaeologists had not been connected with universities. This was so then; it is less so now; but we still have a long way to go before we teach effectively in our British universities the sciences of man. When that time comes prehistory will take its proper place in British education.

But my object in these lectures is not to fulminate against the neglect of prehistory in our educational system; it is rather to discover what sort of picture people have given at different times in the last century – or more – of man's prehistoric past.

It is only too true, as we all know, that history varies with the historian who recounts it, and with the state of development of the subject. We were brought up at school to believe that there were immutable historical facts, and find when we grow up that they are as mutable as the interpretations of those who write about them, and as varying as the models which those writers assume. So it is with prehistory; the prehistory of man has varied very much with the prehistorian and with the state of development of our knowledge, and with the preconceptions brought to bear on the archaeological record as it is being translated into historical contexts. It is fair, therefore, to speak of Worsaae's prehistory, of Gabriel de Mortillet's prehistory, of Gordon Childe's prehistory, of Nazi and Marxist prehistory. It is with these and other ideas of prehistory that we shall be concerned in these lectures, and also the reason behind the various prehistories – reasons which lie partly in the disposition of the prehistorian – those prejudices and preferences which, try as we may, colour our basic thinking as well as our emotional thought, and whose origin no man can clearly tell – and partly in the state of knowledge of the material which the prehistorian is interpreting. The state of the material record can colour and control the prehistorian's interpretative activities without any consideration of his own preconceptions and predispositions.

We have used the word material advisedly, and we must here be clear at the outset of our discussions together what we mean. The material which the prehistorian uses – which he interprets – is, by definition, and by fact, unwritten. It is the unwritten remains of the early past of man, the mute, silent witness of the origins and early development of prehistory – tools, weapons, houses, temples, paintings, tombs, farms, fields, forts, watermills – in a word it is all archaeological material. It is, then, first a record of artifacts, of things made and fashioned by man, and, second, a record of associated features that are not artifacts, such evidence of the flora and fauna that surrounded early man and that he utilized, or his own bones and skin and hair.

The prehistorian is then an archaeologist, indeed has to be an archaeologist, and an archaeologist all the time; so much so that quite often the phrase *prehistoric archaeology* is used synonymously with *prehistory*. For example the Chair of Prehistory at Edinburgh – for that is what it is – now held by Professor Stuart Piggott, and formerly by Professor Gordon Childe, is called the Abercromby Chair of Prehistoric Archaeology. Rather too often one finds people – people who ought to know better – who pretend not to understand the distinction between prehistorian and archaeologist, and of course it would only be splitting very thin hairs indeed to say that there was any difference between a prehistorian and a prehistoric archaeologist. But there is an essential difference between prehistory and archaeology; an archaeologist is a person who studies the material remains of the past with the aim of wresting the facts of history from them, and he can work in any period from the Upper Palaeolithic of the caves to the Late Medieval of the Gothic Cathedrals or the late nineteenth century of the archaeology of disused railways. Sir Alfred Clapham used to say that archaeology began when living memory ended; many others have said it is much later. Each week – or if we are fortunate, twice a week – we see our domestic refuse being carted off and dumped in municipal refuse dumps – a stratified accumulation of gin bottles and tin cans, broken teacups and rotting cabbage stalks for archaeologists of the future to study. The archaeological record – the material remains of the past – starts yesterday when you throw an empty tobacco tin into the wastepaper basket, or this morning when the roadman was shovelling a broken milk bottle into his cart.

There are of course specialized archaeologists who deal with paintings and houses and ecclesiastical architecture. And there is a very curious tradition which is met with in some parts of the museum world, and which I have often had occasion to come across in dealing with the television programme *Animal, Vegetable, Mineral?* that splits up the material remains of the past into archaeological objects, antiques, and bygones. Yet an Italian goffering iron and a seventeenth-century silver tankard are as much archaeology as a La Tène sword or a ruined megalithic tomb. Let me ask you not to be confused in your thinking on this point by books which offer you introductions to archaeology and turn out to provide introductions to prehistory – to a part only of the enormous field which is, properly speaking, archaeology. All material remains are archaeology, but the archaeologist cannot, or should not, usually practise a catholicity in time and space; he must needs specialize and is to be pardoned if he sometimes thinks his specialized interests are the whole of archaeology. It is the archaeologist who specializes in prehistory that is our concern in these lectures. He has been coming into his own very slowly since Daniel Wilson gave him a name in 1851.

I have said that the archaeologist is concerned in wresting facts of historical meaning out of the intractable material left behind, that he is concerned in creating historical contexts out of the material remains. It was not always so with the student of antiquities. Antiquarian studies began in Western Europe with the renaissance of learning. Sixteenth-century scholars in Italy found and studied the classical civilizations of Greece and Rome not only in literature but in archaeology. At the same time, in England, men like William Camden and Humfrey Lhuyd were studying the visible antiquities of Britain. It may well have been that they were impelled to a study of antiquity by the dissolution of the monasteries and the dispersal of the religious libraries, that they sought in the past for the beginnings of the new and flourishing nation of Tudor England. Whatever was the reason, or the sum total of the reasons, there was in England at that time what Camden called a 'back looking curiousity', and although he recognized that there were some 'which wholly contemne and avile this study of Antiquity', he himself felt otherwise. 'In the study of Antiquity (which is always accompanied with dignity,' he wrote, 'and hath a certaine resemblance with eternity), there is a sweet food of the mind well befitting such as are of honest and noble disposition.'

But for many the attraction of antiquities lay in less philosophical channels. The collectors are among our earliest antiquaries. The Earl of Arundel, the Duke of Buckingham, King Charles I, were all collectors; so was John Tradescant, once gardener to Queen Henrietta Maria, and it is his Closet of Curiosities, popularly known at Tradescant's Ark, which formed the nucleus of the Ashmolean Museum. Collecting became something of an obsession, and in his *Polyolbion*, written in 1622, Drayton complains that there was 'nothing esteemed in this lunatique age, but what is kept in cabinets'.

It was the age of the collectors that produced the word *dilettanti* – those who delighted in the arts, and we should not underestimate the aesthetic factor in the development of antiquarianism. The cultivation of taste had a very large influence in the discovery of the past. This aesthetic factor often worked for good in a surprising way. It was Sir William Hamilton's *Antiquités Etrusques, Greques, et Romaines*, published in 1766-7, that inspired the potter Wedgwood with new ideas, and in recognition of this inspiration the Wedgwood works in Staffordshire still bear the name Etruria.

In 1707 a group of men interested in antiquities and history formed themselves into a club. They used to meet in the Young Devil and Bear Taverns in the Strand; and out of this Tavern Society was born the Society of Antiquaries of London, the oldest society of its kind in the world – it received its Royal Charter in 1751 – and second in seniority only to the Royal Society among the learned societies of England. But its members were divided as to why they were studying antiquities: were they impelled by the back-looking curiosity, or was it as collectors or as dilettanti that they came to meetings and contributed papers to the Society's journal *Archaeologia*, first published in 1770? One Fellow, Horace Walpole, had no doubts and fiercely castigated those who had no aesthetic feeling and no discrimination in their study of man's past. The second volume of *Archaeologia* set him off. 'Mercy on us,' he wrote to William Cole, on looking through it, 'what a cartload of bricks and rubbish and Roman ruins they have piled together'; and again, in another letter,

the antiquaries will be as ridiculous as they used to be; and since it is impossible to infuse taste into them, they will be as dry and dull as their predecessors. One may revive what perished, but it will perish again, if more life is not breathed into it than it enjoyed originally . . . Bishop Lyttelton used to torment me with barrows and Roman camps, and I would as soon have attended to the turf graves in our Churchyards. I have no curiosity to know how awkward and clumsy men have been in the dawn of arts or in their decay.

But there were others who had this 'curiosity', even when they might, as we may now, acknowledge the force of some of Walpole's criticism. There are many of us at the present day who are tormented by, and torment others with, Roman camps and hand axes, Mesolithic flints and megalithic tombs. Is our torment necessary and do we do it because we are still inveterate collectors, at a mature age preferring flints and tombs to the stamps and butterflies of our youth, or are we really and honestly historians? We shall see as we go along what our modern idea of prehistory really is. In the eighteenth century there was no agreement. Then Walpole could call the Society of Antiquaries 'the midwives of superannuated miscarriages', Edward Balme could say 'the world calls us old women', and Samuel Foote could have a great success in the Haymarket Theatre in 1772 with a play in the third act of which the Nabob visits the Society of Antiquaries preceded by four black porters bearing the twelve lost books of Livy, a piece of lava from the last eruption of Vesuvius, a box of petrifactions, bones, beetles, and butterflies, and a green chamber-pot described as a sarcophagus or Roman urn dug up from the Temple of Concord. These things could happen then, but at this same time a new awareness of the real purpose of antiquarian study was coming into existence. In 1793 the Reverend James Douglas published his *Nenia Britannica or the Sepulchral History of Great Britain*. It was an account of several hundred barrows which he had excavated. Douglas's digging would not pass modern tests, but his purpose in excavation was clear and sound. 'If the study of antiquity be undertaken in the cause of History,' he wrote in his preface, 'it will rescue itself from a reproach indiscriminately and fastidiously bestowed on works which have been deemed frivolous.'

'In the cause of History': these were Douglas's words and this was the change that was taking place in the late eighteenth and early nineteenth century. The material remains of the past were being studied not by collectors and dilettanti, not because the curious or the beautiful were being cultivated, but by men who were consciously trying to wrest historical facts from the material of archaeology.

In their excavations in Wiltshire, William Cunnington of Devizes and Sir Richard Colt Hoare were trying hard and very consciously to eschew the romantic, acquisitive, or dilettanti approach of their predecessors as antiquaries. In 1803 William Cunnington described himself as digging barrows on Salisbury Plain 'in the hopes of meeting something which might supersede conjecture'. In his *Ancient Wiltshire* Colt Hoare said 'we speak from facts not theory. I shall not seek among the fanciful regions of Romance an origin of our Wiltshire barrows.'

Real prehistory began with men like these striving to understand man's prehistoric past from the surviving material remains of that past. But of course there was speculation about man's prehistory, about his beginning and development before writing, long before prehistoric archaeology began. In a way the theme of this lecture is prehistory before archaeology, and our concern is now with some of the ideas of prehistory that existed before scholars had turned to archaeology as their source. The Greeks, of course, had speculated about early man. In the eighth century B.C. Hesiod in his *Works and Days* speaks of a time in man's past when bronze had not been superseded by iron. Lucretius in his *De rerum natura* asserted that man first used his nails and teeth, and stones and wood and fire, then copper, and still later iron gained in popularity. The Greeks also had other ideas of Ages and Stages in man's past – the Age of Reason, the Golden Age, the Heroic Age for example.

The Christian religion provided an answer to speculations about man's early history. God formed man in his own image on the sixth day of creation. Eve was created from one of Adam's ribs and together they were expelled from the park of Eden bearing Cain and Abel. Adam lived for nine hundred and thirty years. His seventh descendant was Methuselah who lived to be nine hundred and eighty-two years old. Methuselah's grandson was Noah, and it was when this Noah was six hundred years old – almost all the members of this first original family seem to have been extremely long lived – that the Great Deluge of water flooded the earth. From the exact dates provided for these lives many have tried to fix the date of the Flood and of the Creation of Man himself. James Ussher, Archbishop of Armagh, calculated in the early seventeenth century that from the evidence in the Old Testament it was possible to declare that the earth had been created in 4004 B.C. These calculations and dates, published in Ussher's *Annals of the Ancient and New Testaments* (1650), were widely accepted; the year 4004 B.C. was inserted in the margins of the Authorized Version of the Bible where, to quote White's *History of the Warfare of Science with Theology in Christendom*, it was 'soon practically regarded as equally inspired with the sacred text itself'.

Ussher did not say in what part of the year 4004 B.C. he thought the creation of man had taken place. Bede in the eighth century and Vincent of Beauvais in the thirteenth thought that it must have been in the spring. Others favoured 'September at the Equinox' and among them was Dr John Lightfoot, Master of St Catharine's and Vice-Chancellor of the University of Cambridge, who published his *A Few and New Observations on the Book of Genesis, the most of them certain, the rest probable, all harmless, strange and rarely heard of before*, in 1642. Later Dr Lightfoot refined his dating and declared

heaven and earth, centre and circumference, were created all together in the same instant and clouds full of water ... this took place and man was created by the Trinity on October 23, 4004 B.C. at nine o'clock in the morning.

We may perhaps see in these dates and time a prejudice of a Vice-Chancellor for the beginning of an academic year and the beginning of an academic morning, but, at least, Lightfoot did provide an exact and absolute chronology which must have been very comforting.

If you accepted these comfortable dates – and most people did in the late seventeenth and eighteenth century – then the extent of man's prehistory was not long. The civilizations of Greece and Rome had flourished before Christianity, and before them again the empires of the Near East. The four-monarchy system could easily take up a great deal of the time of man on earth; the time before the four world Empires of Assyria, Persia, Greece and Rome did not need to be long, and was surely long enough to fit in whatever archaeological remains were shown to be pre-Roman, pre-Greek, pre-Assyrian, and pre-Persian.

But as one moved away from the four-monarchy area, the gap of time that was prehistory, even on the Ussher–Lightfoot chronology, became larger and larger. In the British Isles there were four thousand yawning years of prehistory before

Julius Caesar and Claudius. What was to be put into these four millennia? Or did Britain have no prehistory? The earliest British antiquaries just invented peoples to fill up this early blank in the record of our island story, but their inventions, as was necessary for their successful adoption, bore some relationship to known historical facts outside the British Isles. Sir Thomas Kendrick, in his *British Antiquity* (1950), has given us a splendid summary of antiquarian speculation about British prehistory from the twelfth to the sixteenth centuries, and I have gone over some of these speculations in my 1954 Rhŷs Lecture to the British Academy, *Who are the Welsh?*

The *Historia Brittonum* of Nennius, written in the ninth century A.D., gave us a prehistory beginning with Brutus, grandson of Aeneas, settling in Britain in the third age of the world and producing the first regular inhabitants of these islands since the Flood. Geoffrey of Monmouth in the twelfth century made Brutus, Prince of Trojan Blood, land in 1170 B.C. at Totnes. This Troynovantian prehistory of Britain certainly flourished right up to the sixteenth century in Britain. Men like Sir John Price, Sir Winston Churchill, William Wynne, Daniel Langhorne, and Robert Sherwood in the seventeenth century were all for Greeks and Trojans in British prehistory. Even as late as 1674 the Oxford *Almanack* had Brute heading the list of kings of Britain; two years later he had been replaced by William the Conqueror.

Other antiquaries preferred a more direct Biblical origin to the Trojans and Greeks. One of these was the Reverend Henry Rowlands, Vicar of Llanrhidian in Anglesey, whose *Mona Antiqua Restaurata* was published in 1723. 'Antiquity recordeth and the consent of nations celebrateth the sons of Japhet to have been the first planters of Europe,' he wrote; Britain was 'peopled by these men very soon after the flood'. Seven years before Rowlands wrote these words in English in his Anglesey rectory another Welshman had published a book called *Drych y Prif Oesoedd* – the mirror of the first ages, and here we find a prehistory of Wales beginning in the Tower of Babel and the invasion of Britain by Gomer, the grandson of Noah.

The Phoenicians were canvassed for our prehistory by those who preferred them to Greeks and Trojans, or to Noah and Japhet. John Twyne, Headmaster of Westminster School, died in 1581; his *De Rebus Albionicis Britannicus atque Anglicis* was published by his son nine years after his death. Twyne brought the Phoenicians to Cornwall looking for tin. He argued that the Welsh word *caer* was Phoenician, that Welsh coracles were Phoenician; so was the dark blood of the Silures – even the dress of the Welsh women in the sixteenth century was, according to Twyne, a survival of an old Phoenician form of dress – though it was of course a provincial survival of English court dress. Samuel Bochart in his *Geographia Sacra* (1646) and Aylett Sammes's *Britannia Antiqua Illustrata* (1676) were full of the Phoenicians and the civilizing role they played in western Europe and particularly the British Isles; and there is no doubt that many people at the present day still think of the Phoenicians as having come to Britain and having affected considerably our early civilization.

Other antiquaries preferred the Lost Tribes of Israel to Phoenicians and Trojans, and, in the nineteenth century, the British Israelites excavated at Tara – Royal Tara – in Ireland searching for the Ark of the Covenant, which they, in all sincerity, believed lay buried there. The Ten-tribists, like the advocates of the Phoenicians, survive to the present day, and I have often been asked in the Welsh countryside – perhaps my surname has something to do with this – whether the Welsh, and therefore, of course, the ancient pre-Roman inhabitants of Britain, are not really the Lost Tribes of Israel.

But it is unquestionably the Druids who became the most popular explanation of our prehistory in pre-archaeological days. It was the antiquary John Aubrey who floated the Druids into our new historical consciousness, and it was in connexion with a monument which is still to many people 'Druidic', and which suffers at midsummer from visitations of modern out-group cultists calling themselves 'Druids' – I refer, of course, to Stonehenge. King James I became interested in Stonehenge and commissioned Inigo Jones to examine it: he prepared a treatise on the subject in 1620 which was not actually published until thirty years later. He declared that it was a Roman temple. In 1663, Dr Carleton, a court physician, insisted that it was built by the Danes for the consecration of their kings. John Webb restored Stonehenge to the Romans. John Twyne and Aylett Sammes naturally made it Phoenician. Bishop Nicholson made it Saxon. Bolton declared it to be the tomb of Boadicea.

> I come in the rear of all [wrote Aubrey], by comparative evidence to give clear evidence that these monuments [Avebury, Stonehenge, and the like] were Pagan temples; which was not made out before; and have also with humble submission to better judgement, offered a probability that they were Temples of the Druids.

I must go on quoting what he says because, though written in the seventeenth century – John Aubrey's dates were 1626–97 – it is most germane to our purpose here of understanding prehistory before archaeology.

> This inquiry, I must confess [he says], is a groping in the dark; but although I have not brought it into clear light, yet can I affirm that I have brought it from an utter darkness to a thin mist, and have gone further in this essay than anyone before me.

Dr Plot, the historian of Staffordshire and the first keeper of the Ashmolean Museum, believed in the Druids, and so did Toland (1670–1722) who wrote a very odd history of the Druids. But it is William Stukeley who is our arch-Druidist, our arch-romantic, and his Druidomania has been admirably portrayed by Professor Stuart Piggott in his biography of him. Stukeley's books on Stonehenge and Avebury appeared in 1740 and 1743, and here he made them Druidic monuments. Indeed as he grew older everything was Druidic. Piggott gives a fine account of how in 1754 Stukeley visited the Princess Dowager in Kent House to discuss what we know now to be a Late Bronze Age hoard of socketed axes and other tools. They talked of Druids, patriarchal religion, oaks, acorns, and mistletoe, and of Stonehenge. Stukeley returned home carrying a branch of oak picked up in the garden – it was acorn-heavy, symbolic. He passed the house of a friend, Mrs Peirson, and by a servant sent in the oak bough as 'a present from the royal Archdruidess, to her sister Druidess'; and his journal goes on 'My Lord Archdruid Bathurst ordered me to meet him at dinner.' As Piggott remarks, 'on this wonderful autumn day everyone was a Druid'.*

What I have been saying will, I hope, bring home to you the problems of the antiquaries of the pre-archaeological period. Everything had to belong to something and to something clearly named and historical. One could not confess failure about the early past of man; it had to be peopled by someone, and it did not really matter a great deal whether they were Danes, Romans, Greeks, Trojans, Noah and Japhet, Israelite tribes, Phoenicians, or Druids. They had to be nominate; they had to be named people to whom one could turn confidently. Here was no time for the innominate uncertainties of modern prehistory.

Even the Egyptians were canvassed as the progenitors of the British – and this well before the days of Rendell Harris, Elliot Smith, and W. J. Perry. Charles Vallancey is a good example of the eccentric antiquaries who cultivated the Egyptians. His dates are 1721–1812; he was an engineer in Ireland and rose to the rank of full General. He wrote on the origins of Irish which he compared with Kalmuck, Punic, the language of the Algonquin Indians, and later with Egyptian, Persian, and Hindustani. One of his books was called *The Ancient History of Ireland proved from the Sanskrit Books*. As the

* S. Piggott, *William Stukeley*, Oxford, 1950, p. 170.

writer of Vallancey's life in the *Dictionary of National Biography* says, a little uncharitably, of Vallancey's writing, 'the facts are never trustworthy and their theories are invariably extravagant'. To Vallancey the Egyptians were all over Ireland and Britain; even the great Irish megalithic tomb of New Grange, dating from perhaps 2000 to 1600 B.C., was a Mithraic temple. He found an inscription on the walls of New Grange which he declared to be partly Cadmean and partly Egyptian, and read it as ' "Angus", the name of an Arch-Druid, or more likely "Anghein", the "Holy Ones" '. Poor Charles Vallancey! he was certainly near the broad lunatic fringes of antiquarian thought. But he had one great merit; his work called forth the wonderful parody published in 1790 under the title of *Eymetomena* or *The Antiquities of Killmackumpshaugh*, and for that we must be eternally grateful.

Vallancey had made New Grange Egyptian. In 1735 Thomas Molyneux, Professor of Physick in the University of Dublin, wrote about this remarkable stone tomb. He was very critical of Irish writers who 'deduce their stock from generations near the flood . . . invent antediluvian stories, and a fable of a niece of Noah himself landing in this island'. For Molyneux, New Grange was a *Danes-Mount* 'raised in honour of some mighty prince or person of the greatest power and dignity in his time'. Forty years later New Grange was visited by Governor Pownall. He drew particular attention to a stone with the engraving which Colonel Vallancey had curiously translated but which Irish archaeologists in later years, like George Coffey, have thought to be a stylized ship motif. Pownall was sure that it was writing and that the 'characters are evidently neither Irish, Punic, nor Saxon'. 'I have persuaded myself,' he goes on, 'that this inscription is Phoenician and contains only numerals,' and was part of a 'marine or naval monument erected at the mouth of the Boyne by some Eastern people to whom the parts of Ireland were well-known'.

But one of the great interests to us in our present inquiry of Governor Pownall is that at the very same time when he is writing in terms of fixed historical named peoples, he also had a wider and more general idea of life in prehistoric times, and was prepared to discuss prehistory in terms of unnamed hypothetical groups of people. In his general account of New Grange published in that very Volume 11 of *Archaeologia* in 1773 which had made Horace Walpole so cross, he writes this interesting long passage which I must quote *in extenso*.

This globe of earth hath, according to the process of its nature, existed under a successive change of forms and been inhabited by various species of mankind, living under various modes of life, suited to that particular state of the earth in which they existed. The face of the earth being originally everywhere covered with wood, except where water prevailed, the first human beings of it were *Woodland-Men* living on the fruits, fish, and game of the forest. To these the land-worker succeeded. He *settled* on the land, became a fixed inhabitant and increased and multiplied. Where-ever the land-worker came, he, as at this day, eat out the thinly scattered race of Wood-Men.

Now, here, in Woodland Men and Land Workers, is an entirely different kind of prehistory from that which dealt in Trojans and Phoenicians and Egyptians. Where did it come from? It seems to me to be part and parcel of the philosophical speculations about the origins and development of man, language, and society associated with what have been called the Scottish primitivists who flourished in the middle and second half of the eighteenth century, and mainly, as their name suggests, in Scotland. Professor Piggott has drawn attention to the appropriateness of that episode in Thomas Love Peacock's *Crochet Castle* when, at the end of a most convivial dinner, Mr McQuedy repeatedly tries to read a paper which begins 'In the infancy of society . . .'.* In the eighteenth century

* *Antiquity*, 1955, p. 153.

Scottish thinkers were interested in the infancy of society, and in the prehistory of man. One who was especially so interested was Thomas Blackwell, who held the Chair of Greek at Marischal College, Aberdeen, from 1723 to 1757.

Blackwell's pupil was James Burnett (1714–99) who took the title of Lord Monboddo when he became a Lord of Session. Monboddo was indeed a strange man; he never sat with his colleagues but always underneath with the clerks. He was an amiable, generous, and kind-hearted man; the learned suppers he gave once a fortnight are famous. In 1780 he started visiting London regularly and there often met and talked with George III. He considered the carriage an engine of effeminacy and idleness so went on horseback with a single servant. There is a story of him hailing a coach during a rainstorm to carry his wig, while he continued to walk. Monboddo's great work *On the Origin and Progress of Language* was published in six volumes between 1773 and 1792, and his *Ancient Metaphysics* in another six volumes between 1779 and 1799. It was in these books that he set out the view that the orang-utan was a class of the human species and its want of speech was accidental. He believed, too, that we were born with tails and that it was a world-wide league of quick-witted midwives who had prevented this great truth from being known hitherto.

Lord Monboddo's contemporaries, not unnaturally, thought him most eccentric and treated his views with the utmost derision. He met Dr Johnson during the latter's tour of the Hebrides, at Monboddo in Kincardineshire. Indeed Monboddo has been described by a contemporary as 'an Elzevir edition of Samuel Johnson'. Johnson himself did not like Monboddo and held him and his views in contempt. He said:

It is a pity to see Lord Monboddo publish such notions as he has done: a man of sense and so much elegant learning. There would be little in a fool doing it; we should only laugh; but when a wise man does it we are sorry. Other people have strange notions, but they conceal them. If they have tails, they hide them; Lord Monboddo is as jealous of his tail as a squirrel.

Now there are two things of especial interest to us here. First, Monboddo had some interesting ideas, of a general philosophical nature, about the origin and development of man. But the second point of interest is the attitude of Dr Johnson who thought not only that Monboddo was silly and odd, but that it was wrong and vain and useless to speculate about such things as the origin of man and society.

Arthur Lovejoy has argued in his discussion of the Scottish primitivists, that Monboddo and Blackwell got their ideas from the medieval notion of an ordained universe of purposeful and unfolding plan – the notion known in the post-medieval world by such names as the Great Chain of Being – a concept in which everything from the lowliest object to man had a place in the framework.* Monboddo and the Scottish primitivists conceived a prehistory out of these philosophical speculations. General Pownall's Woodland Men and Land Workers were part of these philosophical postulates.

Dr Johnson, on the other hand, was sure that such postulates were absurd. Speaking sharply of Monboddo's views, he said:

Sir, it is all conjecture about a thing useless, even if it were known to be true. Knowledge of all kinds is good. Conjecture, as to things useful, is good. But conjecture as to what would be useless to know, such as whether men went upon all fours, is very idle.

There is something quite fundamental here: for Dr Johnson there was no prehistory, there *could* be no prehistory. In the words of the late Stanley Casson:

History to Johnson was recorded history. He could not see further back than the written word. For to him the written word had the value of Holy Writ.†

* On the Great Chain of Being see Arthur Lovejoy, *The Great Chain of Being*, 1933, and C. C. Gillispie, *Genesis and Geology*, New York, 1959.
† S. Casson, *The Discovery of Man*, London, 1939, p. 166.

But could Dr Johnson be blamed? Could he really be blamed for saying:

> All that is really known of the ancient state of Britain is contained in a few pages. We can know no more than what old writers have told us.

What had others to offer? There were the legendary pre-histories of the medieval and post-medieval antiquaries, and there were the philosophical speculations of the Scottish primitivists, possibly as remote from reality as the Golden Ages and Heroic Ages of the Greeks. Admittedly there were antiquaries who were trying to wrest some facts about the past from the material remains they studied, but they were not getting very far; indeed from time to time they confessed that they were in despair.

Sir Richard Colt Hoare had set out with high hopes in his investigations of the Wiltshire barrows but, after ten years' work, was forced to confess 'total ignorance of the authors of these sepulchral memorials'.

> We have evidence [he wrote] of the very high antiquity of our Wiltshire barrows, but none respecting the tribes to whom they appertained, that can rest on solid foundations.

Colt Hoare, thwarted from continental travel as he declared 'by the tyrannous Corsican', had toured Ireland in 1806. In his account of his *Tour in Ireland* published in the following year – and I remind you here that we are dealing with one of the foremost British archaeologists of his time –

> I shall not unnecessarily trespass upon the time and patience of my readers in endeavouring to ascertain what tribes first peopled this country; nor to what nation the construction of this singular monument [he is writing of New Grange] may reasonably be attibuted for, I fear, both its authors and its original destination will ever remain unknown. Conjecture may wonder over its wild and spacious

domains but will never bring home with it either truth or conviction. Alike will the histories of those stupendous temples at AVEBURY and STONEHENGE which grace my native county, remain involved in obscurity and oblivion.

Here was indeed a counsel of despair, and it was felt all over Europe by those who at the end of the eighteenth century and the beginning of the nineteenth were trying to get some ancient history out of what they knew were ancient remains. I always like quoting in this connexion a remark made by Professor Rasmus Nyerup, one of the pioneers of Danish prehistoric archaeology. For years Nyerup had been privately collecting antiquities and had formed them into a small museum at the University of Copenhagen, of which he was librarian. But he had been quite unable to classify them in any significant way, confessing that

everything that has come down to us from heathendom is wrapped in a thick fog; it belongs to a space of time which we cannot measure. We know that it is older than Christendom but whether by a couple of years or a couple of centuries, or even by more than a millennium, we can do no more than guess.

That is where prehistory was at that moment; still at a time of guesses and conjectures – conjecture that will never bring home truth or conviction, the conjecture which Dr Johnson found so idle. The archaeologists, struggling for historical truth, could as yet offer no prehistory – nothing but obscurity, oblivion – thick fog. It was not because they believed in the divine inspiration of Genesis but because of the inadequacy of any other prehistory that learned men even well into the nineteenth century turned to the Genesis account of the Creation, the Fall, and the Flood to explain the origin of man and society, and clutched at the firm dates of Ussher and Lightfoot to give them a secure chronology of the past. The Fall and the Flood of the Fundamentalists would stay as articles of belief

until the growth of archaeology and geology gradually penetrated the obscurity and oblivion which so despairingly
wrapped in fog the prehistoric beginnings of man. We shall
be concerned next with the revolution in thought which took
place between 1810 and 1859 and substituted stratigraphical
geology and systematic archaeology for the Flood and the Fog
of prehistory before archaeology.

CHAPTER TWO

THE BEGINNINGS OF ARCHAEOLOGICAL PREHISTORY

THE 23rd of October is the anniversary of the creation as accurately dated by Bishop Lightfoot. While we realize that many people did not, in the seventeenth and eighteenth centuries, believe in the exact detail of the Ussher–Lightfoot dates, yet the general notion behind them did then condition general thought about man's past. 'Time we may comprehend,' wrote Sir Thomas Browne in the *Religio Medici*, 'tis but five days elder than ourselves, and hath the same Horoscope with the world.' This was in 1635. Time was understood and was short, and this idea of the shortness of man's past and its interpretation in terms of Biblical exegesis was the prevalent way of thought right up to the early nineteenth century. At the end of the eighteenth century there was prevalent what Professor Wood Jones has called 'a most satisfying and spiritually comforting conception of the universe'.* The whole universe had been designed in perfection, and there was the perfect Chain of Being, *L'échelle des êtres*, the *Scala naturae*.

In 1802 William Paley (1743–1805) wrote his *Natural Theology: or Evidence of the Existence and Attributes of the Deity collected from the appearances of Nature*, a task in which he endeavoured, as he says in his preface dedicated to the Bishop of Durham, 'to repair in the study his deficiencies in the Church'. He set out to show that man had only inhabited the world for six thousand years, that the world 'teemed with delighted existence', but had not done so for more than six thousand

* *Design and Purpose*, London, 1942, p. 41.

years, and that it was all a splendid design like a watch, indeed created by God the arch-watchmaker.*

In 1833 the Trustees of the Earl of Bridgewater commissioned authors selected by the President of the Royal Society in consultation with the Archbishop of Canterbury and the Bishop of London to write treatises illustrating and elaborating Paley's *Natural Theology* or the thesis clearly expounded therein – Paley has been described as one of the best writers of textbooks that ever existed. These treatises 'designed to prove that the creation story of Genesis was literally exact and that Noah's ark and the Flood were facts of prehistory', were written by men like Prout and Whewell and Dean Buckland and were published in 1833.

I ask you particularly to remember those two dates; 1802 when Paley's *Natural Theology* was first published and 1833, the year of the *Bridgewater Treatises*. Two years before Paley wrote there was published in Volume XIII of *Archaeologia* a short 'Account of Flint Weapons discovered at Hoxne in Suffolk' by John Frere. The year in which the *Bridgewater Treatises* were published saw also the publication of the third and last volume of Sir Charles Lyell's *Principles of Geology*, the work that really destroyed the Diluvialist geology of the Catastrophists and which was one of the two great formative books in the mind of Charles Darwin as he worked out and developed his theory of evolution.

Three years after the *Bridgewater Treatises*, in 1836, there was published in Copenhagen the first guide-book to the National Museum; it was called *Ledetraad til Nordisk Oldkyndighed*, and it contained an essay on the early monuments and antiquities of the north by Christian Jurgensen Thomsen. In this essay he set out the notion of three prehistoric ages of stone, bronze, and iron which had been implicit in his classification and

* Paley was accused of having plagiarized his watch idea from Bernard Nieuwentyr (1654–1718), a Dutch disciple of Descartes, but it was a fairly widespread analogy.

arrangement of the National Museum. It was these three things – the recognition of man's early tools for what they were and their association with extinct animals, the acceptance of a fluvialist geology, and the acceptance of the three ages of man's prehistory, that enabled a systematic prehistoric archaeology to come into existence, for the Fog to disperse, and the Flood to subside.

It is my concern to discuss these three revolutions in human thought that occurred between Paley's *Natural Theology* and Darwin's *Origin of Species* – in the half-century between 1802 and 1859, of which the rough half-way mark is the *Bridgewater Treatises* of 1833 and the *Principles of Geology* (1830–33). Let us begin with geology because the acceptance of stratigraphy and uniformitarianism was fundamental to progress in geology or archaeology.

1. *The Development of Geology*

It was the last quarter of the eighteenth century which witnessed the birth of geology as a science and this period saw a great cleavage between those who insisted on interpreting the record of the rocks in conformity with Genesis, and those who believed in interpreting the record in terms of present-day natural phenomena. If you had to fit in the record of the rocks to the six thousand years allowed you by the Ussher–Lightfoot interpretation of Mosaic chronology, the natural modern normal process of accumulation and change had to be accelerated. There had to be catastrophes, of which, surely, it was argued, the Flood provided one admirable historical example. Hence the cleavage between the Diluvialists and Catastrophists on one hand and the Fluvialists on the other.

Georges Cuvier (1769–1832), the great French geologist and naturalist, universally regarded as the 'founder of vertebrate palaeontology', held that the record of the rocks could be interpreted correctly only by supposing that there had been a series of great catastrophes, not merely one; and that the

Noachian Flood of Genesis was a record of one of them. He went further and expressly denied the existence of fossilized man in antiquity; he said that such things just could not be. 'The pope of bones' as Cuvier was called had a tremendous reputation in the study of fossils – 'the medals coined by creation' as he called them. His reputation was enormous as a naturalist, and enhanced by tales like the famous one of his visit from the Devil – only it was not the Devil but one of his students dressed up with horns on his head and shoes shaped like cloven hooves. This frightening apparition burst into Cuvier's bedroom when he was fast asleep and declaimed: 'Wake up thou man of catastrophes. I am the Devil. I have come to devour you!' Cuvier studied the apparition carefully and critically and said, 'I doubt whether you can. You have horns and hooves. You only eat plants.'

The man of catastrophes believed in a series of geological revolutions. He knew of the stratigraphical evidence that was being accumulated by people like William Smith in England. William Smith (1769–1839), 'strata Smith' as he is often called, was described by William Sedgwick in 1831 as the recognized 'Father of English Geology'. He drew up a table of thirty-two different strata and found different fossils in each of them. He called fossils not medals of creation, but 'the antiquities of Nature', and the first part of his *Strata Identified by Organized Fossils* was published in 1816. Now Cuvier in France did not deny the existence of these layers but said that they were separated by catastrophes which obliterated certain animals and plants and which were followed by new creations. Cuvier died in 1832, at the moment when he was about to be made Minister of the Interior. His disciples and pupils Brongniaert and d'Orbigny carried on his work and drew up a dogmatic system of twenty-seven successive acts of creation and catastrophes.

In England, the Reverend W. D. Conybeare (1787–1857), a geologist who became Dean of Llandaff, postulated three deluges before that of Noah. Adam Sedgwick (1785–1873), who was Woodwardian Professor of Geology at Cambridge in 1818, was also in favour of the Flood, and so was William Buckland (1784–1856). Buckland was a very strange character and anecdotes about him abound – how he ate the heart of a French king in Sutton Courtenay Church, kept an orang-utan in his rooms at Christ Church, and prepared for Ruskin's breakfast an 'exquisite toast of mice'. He seems to have been a very great field geologist; the tale I most like about him is that, lost on a journey on horseback from Oxford to London, he dismounted, bent down, picked up a handful of soil and said at once, 'Ah, yes, as I guessed, Ealing.' Buckland was appointed Reader in Mineralogy at Oxford in 1813; it has been said that his courses attracted in a high degree the attention and admiration of the University, and very largely contributed to the public recognition of geology as a science by the endowment in 1819 of a Professorship. But by this time Buckland had gone away from Oxford to be Dean of Westminster. In 1823 he published his *Reliquiae Diluvianae: or Observations on the Organic Remains Contained in Caves, Fissures, and Diluvial Gravel and in other Geological Phenomena Attesting the Action of an Universal Deluge*, and, thirteen years later, his *Geology and Mineralogy Considered in Relation to Natural Theology*. That is what he insisted on – a Universal Deluge, and then held that geology proved it. His 1836 book was a summary of geological knowledge as a proof of 'the power, wisdom, and goodness of God as manifested in creation'.

But, very gradually, a powerful opposition was growing to the Catastrophists and flood-men. In 1785 James Hutton (1726–97) published his *Theory of the Earth: or an Investigation of the Laws Observable in the Composition, Dissolution, and Restoration of Land Upon the Globe*. He saw in the deposits of sand, gravel, clay, and limestone the results of the ordinary deposition of sediments together with organic remains under water, i.e. in the rivers or in the seas in the same way as this deposition went on at present. He fully recognized that the greater part of the solid land had once been beneath the sea, but formed in an ordinary, that is to say, a non-catastrophic way. 'No processes are to be employed,' he said, 'that are not natural to the globe; no action to be admitted except those of which we know the principle.' This was the real beginning of the doctrine of uniformitarianism. William Smith had not only assigned relative ages to the rocks by noting their fossil contents, but himself argued for the orderly deposition of strata over a long period of time.

But the man who really weighed the scales in this issue, who really proved the case for the Fluvialists against the catastrophic Diluvialists, was Charles Lyell whose *Principles of Geology* was published, as we have already mentioned, during 1830–3, in three volumes. May I quote here the title of his great work, because it is, in itself, a definition of the doctrine of uniformitarianism. The full title was: *Principles of Geology, being an attempt to explain the former changes of the Earth's surface by reference to causes now in action.* Conybeare, himself a Catastrophist and a Diluvialist, claimed that this work was 'in itself sufficiently important to mark almost a new era in the progress of our science'. Like Darwin's *Origin of Species*, a work which Lyell's book profoundly affected, it was not that the ideas were new; it is that they were set out cogently, clearly, convincingly.

Of course there was considerable criticism when the first volume was published; many leading geologists were against the notion that present conditions were all that one could allow in the past. They may not have wanted catastrophes and floods, but they did think – and it is arguable – that processes might have been more quick in the past than at present. Conybeare said, and was supported by Sedgwick, that these causes 'may have been modified as to the degrees and intensity of their action by the varying conditions under which they may have operated at different periods'. Sir Joseph Prestwich said in 1886 that there was evidence 'that the physical forces were more active and energetic in geological periods than at present'. Lyell himself accepted this point of view gradually; in his third volume in 1833 he said that he had never advocated that 'the existing causes of change have operated with absolute uniformity from all eternity', although sometimes it did look as if he had done this. It is true that he did change the title of his great work; the title of the eleventh edition of 1872 was *Principles of Geology or the Modern Changes of the Earth and its Inhabitants Considered as illustrative of Geology*.

But the change in title was really only a demonstration of a change in emphasis and bias by the extreme uniformitarians. Gradually uniformitarianism had become the way of official geological thinking. Eventually even Buckland and Sedgwick had to abandon their Diluvialist and Catastrophist views. Buckland's former teacher, John Kidd, gave one of the *Bridgewater Treatises*; it was on *The Adaption of External Nature to the Physical Condition of Man*, and was published in 1833, the same year as the third volume of Lyell's *Principles*. It is worth quoting extensively from what John Kidd said.

Time was also [he wrote], and indeed with the last century, when the shells and other organic remains which are embedded in the chalk and other solid strata, were considered to be the remains and proofs of the Mosaic deluge; and yet at the present day, without any fear of injuring the credibility of the Scriptures, they are admitted very generally to have been deposited anteriorly to the Mosaic deluge. And who will venture to say, in the infancy of a science like geology, that the same change of opinion may not happen with respect to the organic remains of the grave beds and caverns ... by far the greater number of the organic remains of the gravel, as of the caverns, belong to species not known now to exist.

That was the crux of the matter; the moment you accepted the doctrine of uniformitarianism, in however liberal a form, you immediately drew attention to the fact that long before 4004 B.C. there existed animal life – 'organic remains in the

gravels and caverns', as Kidd had said, choosing his words carefully, 'not known now to exist'. That is the real relevance of all
this to our present story; it is not merely that uniformitarianism revolutionized scientific thought, or that stratigraphy
produced an interpretation of the earth's surface which is
fundamental to all archaeology; it is that already human fossils
were being found in association with organic remains belonging to species not known to exist at the present. The Flood was
disappearing, and the Fog was being dissipated, because here
at last was proof of the antiquity of man.

2. *The Discovery of Early Man*

I have just said that human fossils were found in association
with the remains of extinct animals. These fossils were of two
kinds – physical fossils, that is to say the actual remains of early
men, and cultural fossils, that is to say the remains of tools
made and fashioned by man. By definition man is the tool-
using and tool-making animal who walks erect, and by definition no animal is human who has no artifacts. Apes can join
together two sticks so that they can get at a banana out of their
unaided reach, but apes do not make tools. When, therefore,
we find fashioned implements we are, by definition, in the pre-
sence of men, just as much as if we had found a skeleton which
could be classified as human.

Now what we know these days to be humanly fashioned
tools of stone had been found centuries before the publication
of the *Principles of Geology*, but for long they had been explained away as thunderbolts, fairy arrows, elfshot. Ulisses
Aldrovandi in the mid seventeenth century described stone
tools as 'due to an admixture of a certain exhalation of thunder
and lightning with metallic matter, chiefly in dark clouds,
which is coagulated by the circumfused moisture and con-
glutinated into a mass (like flour with water) and subsequently
indurated by heat, like a brick', and these rather surprising
words were written by a man who has been described as the

greatest zoologist of the Renaissance period. Tollius, at about the same time, claimed chipped flints to be 'generated in the sky by a fulgurous exhalation conglobed in a cloud by the circumposed humour'.

Others, however, had already more intelligent views of the nature of stone tools. Mercati, as early as the end of the sixteenth century, had agreed that the so-called thunderbolts were the weapons of a primitive folk ignorant of a knowledge of metallurgy. Sir William Dugdale in his *History of Warwickshire* published in 1650 declared that these stone objects were 'weapons used by the Britons before the art of making arms of brass or iron was known'. Dr Robert Plot, who was the first keeper of the Ashmolean Museum, said in his *History of Staffordshire* (1686) that he agreed with Dugdale, and later, de la Payrere was giving it as his view that the so-called thunderbolts were really the tools of some early and pre-Adamitic race. The year before the publication of Plot's *History of Staffordshire* a megalithic tomb was discovered and excavated at Cocherel near Dreux in the valley of the Eure. It was the first megalithic tomb ever to be excavated with any semblance of care in Western Europe; it belonged to what we should now call the Paris Basin type of gallery grave. Accounts of this excavation were published in 1719 and 1722; what concerns us here is the use and interpretation which these early eighteenth-century scholars made of the polished axes from this tomb. The Abbé of Cocherel had no doubt that the stones were in fact stone tools: he thought they were implements like those used by the American Indians in the early eighteenth century. And Dom Bernard de Montfaucon in his *L'Antiquité expliquée et représentée en figures* (it was published in English translation in 1722) decided that the unburnt bodies in the tomb belonged to 'some barbarous Nation, that knew not yet the Use either of Iron or of any metal'. Incidentally there is here a very clear and early idea of the existence of a stone age in the early past of man. We shall mention this realization again later on; at the moment it is the polished stone objects found with the unburnt skeletons that concern us.

But the acceptance of the view that stone tools were in fact the artifacts of early man took a very long time to be achieved. In 1766 Charles Lyttelton, Bishop of Carlisle, read to the Society of Antiquaries of London a paper on stone hatchets – it is published in *Archaeologia* for 1773. In this Lyttelton declared: 'There is not the least doubt of these stone instruments having been fabricated in the earliest times and by barbarous people, before the use of iron or other metals was known.' He compared them with examples from France and Mexico, and decided they were Ancient British; 'the most ancient remains existing at this day of our British ancestors,' he said, 'and probably coeval with the first inhabitants of this island.'

That was a fine phrase: 'coeval with the first inhabitants'. It begged one big question: how early were the first inhabitants? The problem came to the forefront when these stone objects, now accepted as cultural fossils of man, were found with organic remains belonging to species not known now to exist. The first find of this kind that we know about was made at the end of the seventeenth century in London; it was made in Gray's Inn Lane by a London apothecary and antique dealer called Conyers. In ancient deposits he found a stone axe and with it bones, which, after much thought, he decided were those of an elephant – but which in fact may very well have been those of a mammoth. Conyers declared that the Ancient Britons of those days had not then known the use of metal and had to use stone tools. His views were laughed at and when his friend John Bagford described this Gray's Inn Lane find in 1715, while he accepted the association of elephant and stone tool, he thought that it was a Roman elephant – a Claudian import.

At the end of the eighteenth century another man faced the same problem and resolutely refused to explain away what he had found. This man was John Frere and he had sent his views to the Secretary of the Society of Antiquaries in 1797 as I have already mentioned; these were really overlooked for sixty years until discoveries in the Somme gravels and in South Devon proved beyond all doubt the coeval existence of man and extinct animals. On 22 June 1797 John Frere wrote to the Secretary of the Society of Antiquaries enclosing some flint implements found at Hoxne, near Diss, in Suffolk; his letter is printed in *Archaeologia* for 1800 and it is, as Dr Joan Evans says in her *History of the Society of Antiquaries*, 'a land-mark in the development of prehistory'. *VI. Kindergarten begins,*

This is what John Frere said of his flint implements: 'If not particularly objects of curiosity in themselves . . . must, I think, be considered in that light, from the situation in which they were found.' They were Acheulian hand axes as we would now call them, and they were found twelve feet below the surface of the ground in the bottom layer of some undisturbed strata; and here they were associated with the bones of extinct animals. Frere described them, very properly: 'They are, I think,' he wrote, 'evidently weapons of war, fabricated and used by a people who had not the use of metals,' and, he adds, 'the situation in which these weapons were found may tempt us to refer them to a very remote period indeed, even beyond that of the present world' (Plate 1).

The Society of Antiquaries recorded that 'thanks were returned to our worthy member Mr Frere for this curious and most interesting communication', but it was soon forgotten. It is true that at the beginning of the nineteenth century archaeologists were now getting used to the idea that there were such things as stone tools and they were feeling their way towards the idea of a Stone Age in the past of man. But that was not the historical importance of John Frere and his communication to the Antiquaries. His importance was that he realized the significance not only of the tools *qua* tools but of their situation in undisturbed strata and together with extinct animals. 'Objects of curiosity . . . from the situation in which they were found . . . a situation which may tempt us to refer them to a period even beyond that of the present world.'

That remote period '*beyond that of the present world*' was, despite the fact that John Frere's modest yet most percipient remarks were forgotten, coming nearer to recognition as a fact: one of the first facts in a prehistory based on archaeology. In 1828, Tournal, the curator of the Narbonne Museum, published discoveries he had made in the Grotte de Bize near Narbonne, where he had found human bones associated with extinct animals. Actually this was not the first such association to be described. In 1771 Johann Friedrich Esper, a priest, was digging a cave at Gaylenreuth near Bamberg in the German Jura and he found cave bear and other extinct animals associated with human bones. He published his finds in 1774 and asked himself this question regarding the human bones: 'Did they belong to a Druid or to an Antediluvian or to a Mortal Man of more recent times?' and concluded: 'I dare not presume without any sufficient reason these human members to be of the same age as the other animal petrifactions. They must have got there by chance together with them.'

That was it. *Must* have got there *by chance*; there was *no sufficient reason* to think otherwise. Yet the reasons began to accumulate in the second quarter of the nineteenth century. It was not only Tournal at the Grotte de Bize but other French geologists like Christol, Dumas, and Pitre. And spurred on by these southern French discoveries Schmerling worked in the caves at Engihoul near Liège, the most famous of which was Engis. Here he found seven human skulls, many artifacts, some of them associated with the skeletons of rhinoceros and mammoth. 'There can be no doubt,' wrote Schmerling, 'that the human bones were buried at the same time and by the same cause as the other extinct species.' Nobody believed Schmerling; indeed few bothered to notice his work at the time.

The same fate befell the work of a Roman Catholic priest,

Father J. MacEnery, who was excavating in Kent's Cavern at Torquay from 1824 to 1829. Here, in this famous cave, he found the remains of extinct animals associated with flint implements under the stratified unbroken floor of stalagmite of the cavern. He communicated his find to Dean Buckland and other geologists while preparing his discoveries for publication. Dean Buckland insisted that MacEnery was wrong. He said that the Ancient Britons, whose artifacts MacEnery had found in Kent's Cavern, had scooped ovens in the stalagmite and that their implements had penetrated the layer of stalagmite only through these holes. In vain did MacEnery protest that there were no such holes, that no such ovens had been scooped out; yet out of deference to the views of Buckland, MacEnery abandoned his idea of publishing his discoveries at Kent's Cavern.

At the very time when MacEnery was working in Kent's Cavern, Dean Buckland himself was having trouble in interpreting the finds in the Goat's Hole Cave at Paviland on the Gower coast of Glamorgan. Here he had found the skeleton of a young man – the so-called Red Lady of Paviland – associated with Palaeolithic flint implements. There was no real doubt of the association, but Buckland could not bring himself to accept it – the skeleton, he said, 'was clearly not coeval with the antediluvian bones of the extinct species', and he dated it to the Romano-British period.

Admittedly Buckland was fighting for the Catastrophists, and it was not until the battle between the old and the new geology was over that the evidence of the antiquity of man was accepted. The third volume of Lyell's *Principles of Geology* was published in 1833; four years later a customs official of Abbeville, by name Jacques Boucher de Crêvecoeur de Perthes, began collecting flints from the Somme gravels. They were roughly chipped flints of the kind which nowadays we call Abbevillian: he called them *haches diluviennes*. In 1838 he showed some of them at Abbeville, and in the next year in

Paris; and in that year he published the first of five volumes of his book called *De la Création; essai sur l'origine de la progression des êtres*. His critics laughed at him, but he went on, undaunted, and in 1847 published the first volume of a three-volume work entitled *Antiquités Celtiques et Antédiluviennes*. The title should be noted: his axes were no longer *diluviennes* they were *antédiluviennes*. He found he could no longer explain the association of human artifacts and extinct animals in the Somme gravels by the Diluvial theory.

Very slowly the French came round to de Perthes's point of view. In 1858 an Englishman, Falconer, visited Abbeville, saw the chipped flints and thought that Boucher de Perthes's claims were right. He returned to England and told his opinion to John Prestwich and John Evans, urging them to visit the Somme gravels and see for themselves. This they did in the following year.

Meanwhile a new enthusiast had been excavating at Kent's Cavern, Torquay. He was William Pengelly, a local school-master and a private coach, who was fascinated by geology. He found that his work was demonstrating what MacEnery had demonstrated years before but no one had believed, namely that man was contemporary in south Devon with extinct animals. But it was not until a neighbouring cave, the Windmill Hill Cave at Brixham, was excavated that the scientific world was prepared to accept this remarkable south Devon evidence. From the summer of 1858 to that of 1859 Pengelly dug in the Brixham cave; he found flint tools associated with extinct animals in the cave earth 'on which lay a sheet of stalagmite from three to eight inches thick, and having within and on it relics of lion, hyaena, bear, mammoth, rhinoceros and reindeer'. These were careful excavations conducted by William Pengelly on behalf of a committee of the British Association; it was not possible any more to talk about ovens scooped in the stalagmite by ancient Britons. The 'sufficient reasons' demanded by Esper were here.

When John Evans crossed over to Abbeville to visit Boucher de Perthes he wrote in his diary:

Think of their finding flint axes and arrowheads at Abbeville in conjunction with bones of Elephants and Rhinoceroses 40 ft below the surface in a bed of drift. In this bone cave in Devonshire . . . they have found arrowheads among the bones and the same is reported of a cave in Sicily. I can hardly believe it. It will make my ancient Britons quite modern if man is carried back in England to the days when Elephants, Rhinoceroses, Hippopotamuses and Tigers were also inhabitants of the country.

In a very short while John Evans discovered that what he could hardly believe had, however hardly, to be believed. This is what he said at Abbeville:

The flat axes and implements found among the beds of gravel . . . evidently deposited at the same time with them – in fact the remains of a race of men who existed at the time when the deluge or whatever was the origin of these gravels took place.

Prestwich and John Evans returned to England from the Somme: on 26 May 1859 Prestwich read a paper to the Royal Society, and after it Evans spoke of the flints; on 2 June John Evans spoke to the Society of Antiquaries and said:

This much appears to be established beyond doubt, that in a period of antiquity remote beyond any of which we have hitherto found traces, this portion of the globe was peopled by man.

Later that year, the *annus mirabilis* as it has been called, Sir Charles Lyell as president of the Geological Section of the British Association meeting at Aberdeen said that he was now 'fully prepared to corroborate the conclusions . . . recently laid before the Royal Society by Mr Prestwich'.

The antiquity – the great antiquity – of man was at last accepted; the flood had gone, the fog was being penetrated; and prehistory, as the first stage of man's history, was emerging at last. Indeed two years before these solemn pronouncements in London and Aberdeen, prehistoric man had himself emerged. In 1857 the long bones and skull-cap of a man-like being was discovered at Neanderthal in Prussia. Schaafhausen, who first described these remains, said that the Neanderthal skeleton belonged to a 'barbarous and savage race' and regarded it 'as the most ancient memorial of the early inhabitants of Europe'. Others disagreed, saying that the Neanderthal skeleton was that of a pathological idiot. But it did not really matter if as yet the anatomical fossils of prehistoric man were accepted; the cultural fossils had been. By 1859 Pengelly in Devonshire and Boucher de Perthes in the Somme had proved the antiquity of man – if you accepted the uniformitarian principles of Lyell, and most people were doing this by the sixties.

Dean Buckland's vigorous refusal to accept the evidence from Kent's Cavern and Paviland was, by the sixties, as outmoded as the Deluge itself, which he had defended for so long. Another flood had swept away the Noachian Catastrophists, the flood of evidence which, from the south of France to the Somme, from Liège to Britain, had demonstrated that man was indeed antediluvian and that the six thousand years from 4004 B.C. to the present day could not contain his prehistory as it was slowly being revealed in the archaeological record.

3. The Three Ages of Man

While geologists were disputing the antiquity of man in the gravels of western Europe, historians and museum curators in northern Europe were postulating stages in the prehistory of man which at long last penetrated the despairing fog of which men like Rasmus Nyerup and Richard Colt Hoare had complained. I have already quoted the words of Professor Nyerup:

Everything that has come down to us from heathendom is wrapped in a thick fog; it belongs to a space of time which we cannot measure. We know that it is older than Christendom, but whether by a couple of years or a couple of centuries, or even by more than a millennium, we can do no more than guess.

Actually, for some while before he wrote those despairing words in 1806 there had been hints of how archaeologists could do more than guess at classifying the material remains of the past. More and more people were beginning to recognize the existence of stone tools and to see them as relics of a time when men did not know of the use of metal. They argued on two grounds, first that people would surely not be so stupid as to use only stone tools, if they possessed more efficient tools of bronze and iron. Secondly they argued from the existence of contemporary savage communities in North America and the Pacific who were in a stone age.

In 1807, the year after he had published a book advocating the formation of a National Danish Museum of Antiquities, Professor Nyerup was made Secretary of a Royal Committee set up 'for the Preservation and Collection of National Antiquities'. The Committee was charged to form a national Museum of Antiquities. In 1816 Nyerup was succeeded as Secretary by Christian Jurgensen Thomsen, who was also made the first curator of the National Museum. Thomsen's first task was to arrange the growing collections in some sort of order; this he did by classifying them into three ages of Stone, Bronze, and Iron. His classification was clearly set out in the guide-book to the National Museum – the *Ledetraad til Nordisk Oldkyndighed* published in Copenhagen in 1836 and translated into English in 1848.

Thomsen's idea of three technological ages or stages in man's material cultural past was soon being used in Sweden, and in Germany, where indeed it may have been independently invented.* It was really a very simple idea, when we look back at it now; merely that before he learnt the use of metals man had lived in a stone age, and that even when he had learnt the use of metals, he first used copper or bronze, and only later

---

* On this *see* G. E. Daniel, *The Three Ages*, 1943, and *A Hundred Years of Archaeology*, 1950; and H. J. Eggers, *Einführung in die Vorgeschichte*, Munich, 1959.

learnt to deal with iron ores. A simple idea, yes; but one which immediately gave some chronological depth to man's past.

And it was not merely an idea, or a system for museum classification. Soon excavations in the Danish bogs and the Swiss lake-dwellings afforded stratigraphical proof of the succession of the three ages. As the idea and its stratigraphical demonstration passed to western Europe archaeologists began to see that the artifacts which characterized Thomsen's Stone Age were different from those found in the Somme gravels, and the Devon caves, and they began to think in terms of two Stone Ages – an earlier Stone Age of chipped stones, and a later Stone Age of polished stone. It was an Englishman, Sir John Lubbock (later Lord Avebury), who coined the words Palaeolithic and Neolithic for these two successive ages; this was in his *Prehistoric Times* published in 1865. Three years later, in the tenth edition of his *Principles of Geology*, Sir Charles Lyell is using these phrases. Early man was now thought of as living through four historical – or perhaps rather prehistorical – stages: the Palaeolithic, Neolithic, Bronze, and Early Iron Ages.

Of course there was opposition to the acceptance of these ideas. John Kemble, in 1857, said that the Three-Age system would 'betray us into grave historical errors' and lead us 'into an historical *reductio ad absurdum*'. Even in 1866 the *Guide to the Exhibition Rooms* of the British Museum refers to the Stone, Bronze, and Iron period 'of the Northern Antiquaries', and to 'the order corresponding to that of the supposed introduction of such materials into this country'. Thomas Wright, the Secretary of the Ethnological Society, was strongly opposed to the Three-Age idea. All bronzes were Roman, he declared: and, as for the Stone Age, 'there may have been a period when society was in so barbarous a state that sticks or stones were the only implements with which men knew how to furnish themselves', but he doubted, he said, 'if the antiquary has yet found any evidence of such a period'.

But, gradually, this opposition disappeared. By the late sixties prehistory was actually in existence; the word itself, first in Daniel Wilson's *Prehistoric Annals of Scotland*, soon became current. By 1865 the idea of a prehistory of man was so far advanced that Sir John Lubbock could produce a popular book called *Prehistoric Times* which became a best-seller.

The fog and the flood had at last gone: and in their place was stratigraphical geology, the antiquity of man, and the belief in the three ages of Stone, Bronze, and Iron. An archaeological idea of prehistory had come into existence.

VIII Elementary School Graduation — End of Infancy & childhood of the discipline. Beginning of Adolescence.

CHAPTER THREE

THE VICTORIANS AND PREHISTORY

IN the second lecture I tried to show how the legendary pre-history of pre-archaeological days was gradually replaced in the nineteenth century by an archaeological prehistory based on stratigraphical geology, the belief in the antiquity of man, and the three successive stages of Stone, Bronze, and Iron. This took place between 1807 when the Danish Commission was set up, and 1859 when the existence of stone tools coeval with extinct animals in Devon and on the Somme was publicly acclaimed in London and elsewhere. Archaeological prehistory, as distinct from legendary antiquarian prehistory, was in existence by the sixties of the nineteenth century, and Sir John Lubbock's *Prehistoric Times*, first published in 1865, was a best-seller. Incidentally, it went on being a best-seller for half a century: the seventh edition was published in 1913, a few months after the death of Lord Avebury (as Sir John Lubbock then was), and when I went up to Cambridge as an undergraduate in 1932, mint copies of the seventh edition were for sale on the shelves of Heffer's and Bowes & Bowes.

Let us now analyse the sort of idea of prehistory which was being put out between the first and last editions of *Prehistoric Times* – between 1865 and 1913: in a word to answer the question: what was the Victorian idea of prehistory?

Well, in the first place, it was a notion based on the great antiquity of man, and was firmly based on the acceptance of a very long past for man that could not be cabined and confined within the chronologies set out in the Bible. I realize that Lubbock's *Prehistoric Times* was published when Queen Victoria had been on the throne for nearly half of her long reign of sixty-four years, and that perhaps this chapter should be entitled 'The Later Victorians and Prehistory' rather than 'The Victorians and Prehistory'. From the thirties to the sixties of the nineteenth century the acceptance of the great antiquity of man, as we have seen, was slow. The striking and oft-quoted phrase 'a rose-red city, half as old as time' which John William Burgon wrote in 1845, was not, as I thought as a schoolboy, a flight of poetic fancy. To Burgon and to many early Victorians time *was* only six thousand years old, and he literally meant Petra to be half that time in age. Then we must never forget that the Mosaic chronology was accepted by many because they sincerely thought that Moses was separated by only a few generations of oral tradition from Adam and the creation of man and the world. George Rawlinson, in the Bampton Lecture for 1859 – that famous year – said in all seriousness that Moses's mother Jochebed had probably met Jacob who could have known Noah's son Shem. Shem, he went on, and there is no doubting his sincerity, was probably acquainted with Methuselah, who had been for 243 years a contemporary of Adam. And Adam was the first man, made on the sixth day after that great day when time began.

Very gradually the early Victorian fundamentalist chronology was replaced by the belief in a remote past for man. On this very issue the first words of Lubbock's *Prehistoric Times* were bold, arresting, clear. 'The first appearance of man in Europe,' he said, 'dates from a period so remote that neither history nor tradition can throw any light on his origin or mode of life.' This was only six years after George Rawlinson's speculations about Moses.

James Cowles Prichard (1786–1848) was one of our earliest British anthropologists. He spent the greater part of his life as a physician in Bristol. His two great works are *Researches into the Physical History of Man* which appeared between 1836 and 1847, and *The Natural History of Man* which came out in 1843. In the *Researches* he says very clearly:

Many writers who have been by no means inclined to raise objec-
tions against the authority of the Sacred Scriptures ... have felt
themselves embarrassed by the shortness of the interval between the
Noachic Deluge and the period at which the records of various
nations commence, or the earliest date to which their historical
memorials lead us back.

There really was not enough time, Prichard argued, on the
short Ussher chronology, for the historical events of the world
and for the development of the diversity of the human races.
Others argued that the diversity of language demanded a long
human past. All these arguments – the archaeological, the
argument from physical anthropology, and the argument
from language – demanded a long past for man. Gradually, in
the face of these arguments, the Victorians abandoned the
struggle in defence of 4004 B.C.

There remained the problem: how old was man? If time
was really longer than six thousand years, if the world had a
new horoscope, what was man's position in this? Morlot in
Switzerland, calculating from the thickness of deposits near
Geneva, decided that the Stone Age began seven thousand
years ago. Gilliéron got to much the same figures elsewhere
in Switzerland. It looked as if the Stone Age in Switzerland –
and by this Morlot and Gilliéron meant the Neolithic – was at
least six to seven thousand years old. Arguments from the
thickness and rate of formation of deposits are notoriously
difficult – at the same time as the Swiss calculations were being
made a Mr Horner in Egypt calculated that the Neolithic began there thirteen thousand years ago – but they were of some
help.

If the Neolithic was so old, what was the age of the Palaeolithic which lay back of the Neolithic, stretching away to the
beginning of man? Sir Charles Lyell was prepared to say that
the Somme deposits with their flint implements, mammoth,
and hyena were not less ancient than 100,000 years ago; and
that the Quaternary Ice Age took 220,000 years. Sir Joseph

Prestwich on the other hand wanted only 20,000 years for the Palaeolithic, while Gabriel de Mortillet estimated the beginning of the Old Stone Age as 230,000 to 240,000 years. It all was, as Prestwich said, 'a curious and interesting problem' but not one about which the Victorian geologists and archaeologists could do more than guess. Geochronology was a product of twentieth-century archaeology and Carbon-14 dating is only a matter of the last decade. All that was certain in the late Victorian idea of prehistory was that man was old and that his prehistoric beginnings went back before the Noachian deluge and before 4004 B.C.

The second certainty in the Victorian outlook was that prehistory was no longer a matter of guesswork. It was a matter of scientific deduction; a new discipline which could provide clear and certain answers had arrived. 'Of late years,' declared Lubbock proudly on the first page of *Prehistoric Times*,

a new branch of knowledge has arisen, a new Science has ... been born among us, which deals with times and events far more ancient than any which have yet fallen within the province of the archaeologist. ... Archaeology forms the link between geology and history.

Others did not share Lubbock's assurance that they had at last discovered the key to the prehistoric past; they felt with Palgrave that

we must give it up, the speechless past; whether fact or chronology, doctrine or mythology; whether in Europe, Asia, Africa or America; at Thebes or Palenque, on Lycian shore or Salisbury Plain; lost is lost; gone is gone for ever.

A more hopeful view was being taken by those who found themselves living through a period of great discoveries in prehistoric archaeology. It was only three years after the publication of *Prehistoric Times* – nearly ninety years ago, in 1868 – that Heinrich Schliemann began excavating in Ithaca, and three years later, at Hissarlik, that he achieved that ambition which had fired him through all his life as a business man in Russia and America, an ambition first kindled when he saw a picture in Jarrer's *Universal History*. In 1871 he found Troy; and Homer was attested archaeologically. Even if the splendid gold objects from Troy II which Schliemann's beautiful young Greek wife Sophie smuggled through the Turkish customs beneath her voluminous skirts, are not now thought to be, as Schliemann claimed, the Treasure of Priam, to the world of the seventies of last century he had, by digging in the ground, made Homer come alive in the dusty hillside of the Troad and later at Mycenae. He had created a fresh chapter in the human past, had himself written prehistory, and demonstrated with overwhelming effectiveness that we must not give it up, that the speechless past could speak, that lost is not lost, that gone is not gone for ever (Plate 2).

This of course, as we now see it, is one of the excitements of archaeological prehistory, that the past which seemed for ever gone can be brought back by the skilled use of archaeological reconnaissance, excavation, and interpretation. We are now accustomed to learn of whole civilizations being recovered from the speechless past – the Minoan and Harappan are two that come immediately to mind. We are even accustomed by now to recover the faces of the past: the dead in the Scythian barrows at Pazyrik and in the Danish peat-bog at Tollund (Plate 6) live again after hundreds of years. But these enormous possibilities had to be learned, and the apprehension by the scholars and public of the seventies that Troy and Mycenae could be made to live again by the spade is one of the great moments of the development of an idea of prehistory.

In 1875 Schliemann came to London and read a paper to the Society of Antiquaries of London on his remarkable discoveries. The discussion was opened by W. E. Gladstone who had himself published, in 1858, a book entitled *Studies on Homer and the Homeric Age*. In this book there was no mention of prehistoric archaeology or indeed of any possibility that anything other than literary criticism could illuminate the problem of Homer. Yet by the time, less than twenty years later, when he is speaking to the Society of Antiquaries, the existence and relevance of prehistory were very much in his mind.

When many of us who are among the elders in this room were growing up [said Mr Gladstone], the whole of the prehistoric times lay before our eyes like a silver cloud covering the whole of the lands that, at different periods of history, had become so illustrious and interesting; but as to their details we knew nothing. Here and there was a shadowy, an isolated glimmer of light let in. . . . Now we are beginning to see through this dense mist and the cloud is becoming transparent, and the figures of real places, real men, real facts are slowly beginning to reveal to us their outlines.

Now what were these real places, real men, real facts which, Mr Gladstone claimed, were at last appearing by the end of the third quarter of the nineteenth century? They were, very briefly, of three kinds; first, they were facts about the early days of the great known historical civilizations – the early days of Greece and Rome, of Mesopotamia and of Egypt. Secondly they were facts about cultures and civilizations which were hitherto unknown – the Hittites for example and the early civilizations of America. In the third place they were facts about the development of man's culture before the historic civilizations or in areas alongside the historic civilizations.

The framework for the prehistoric culture sequence had been provided by the Danish Three Age system of Thomsen as modified by Lubbock into the Four Ages of the Palaeolithic, Neolithic, Bronze, and Iron Ages. But, gradually, even this framework was too broad and general, and a division of the four stages began to be made. The Palaeolithic was divided into varying stages with names like Chellean, Acheulian, Mousterian, Solutrean, Magdalenian. In Sweden Oscar Montelius divided the Neolithic into four numbered periods and the Bronze Age into five such. The Iron Age was divided in a variety of ways of which Hallstatt and La Tène were the two best-known divisions and these were soon widely adopted.

As these divisions and subdivisions were being made, people began to ask: what precisely do they mean? Were they universal, that is to say were they stages of human culture through which everyone passed? Was there a single uniform prehistory of man from the Chellean to La Tène and if so, how did this prehistorical development come about? Just as there had been biological evolution, was there also a natural cultural evolution leading through various stages up to civilization?

It was surely not unnatural in an age which had, with some difficulty, accepted the idea of evolution in the biological world for many to think that cultural evolution succeeded to biological evolution and that when man appeared on the scene, when an animal arrived which made tools – extracorporeal limbs as they have been called – the process of evolution continued. The doctrines of social evolution which Herbert Spencer and others were setting out and which were discussed by the late Professor Gordon Childe when he gave the Josiah Mason lectures here in Birmingham three years ago,* seemed to provide a clear interpretation of the prehistoric record which the archaeologists were studying.

In 1867 the great international exhibition was held in Paris; for the first time ever in such an international exhibition there were displayed prehistoric collections, mainly in the 'Galerie de l'histoire du travail'. These were collections of material from all over Europe and from Egypt. As Gabriel de Mortillet said of these collections, it was the first time that prehistory was able to show itself '*d'une manière solennelle et générale. Eh bien, cette première manifestation a été pour eux un triomphe complet.*'

There was, by the way, no prehistory in the Great Exhibi-

* V. Gordon Childe, *Social Evolution*, London, 1951.

tion in Hyde Park in 1851. In response to repeated requests Gabriel de Mortillet wrote a guide to the prehistoric collections at the Paris Exposition of 1867. It was called *Promenades préhistoriques à l'Exposition Universelle*. At the end of this guide he summarized what he thought were the lessons that had so far emerged from the discipline of prehistoric scholarship. He printed them in capital letters as the last words in his book and they were LOI DU PROGRÈS DE L'HUMANITÉ, LOI DU DÉVELOPPEMENT SIMILAIRE, and the third: HAUTE ANTIQUITÉ DE L'HOMME. X. Young adulthood.

About the third of these conclusions there was no doubt. The late Victorians believed in the antiquity of man although they could not agree on an absolute chronology. But there was not really agreement about the other two laws which had as their keynotes the ideas of Parallel Cultural Evolution and Progress. There were many who agreed with de Mortillet when he declared, passionately, after conducting his tour of the collections in the Paris Exposition, 'It is impossible any longer to doubt the great law of the progress of man.' These were indeed the sort of words which an archaeologist might have been repeating from Herbert Spencer who in 1850 had been saying, 'Progress is not an accident but a necessity. It is a fact of nature.' It began to look to some as if prehistoric archaeology was confirming the philosophical and sociological speculations of the mid-nineteenth-century scholars. Gabriel de Mortillet, however much his views were influenced by the current beliefs in progress and evolution, was in fact making an observation from the archaeological record. Prehistory, in the idea which many Victorians had of it, was a record of progress and evolution. This was certainly to many the interpretation of the real facts and the real places which Mr Gladstone had seen appearing in his lifetime.

Mr Gladstone had spoken to the Society of Antiquaries in 1875. This was the year in which the Germans began digging at Olympia, a fact which many, and not unreasonably, regard as the beginning of modern scientific techniques in archaeology. This was also the year in which Marcelino de Sautuola began digging in the cave of Altamira in the Cantabrian Mountains of Spain. Five years later Flinders Petrie began excavating in Egypt and the modern period of Near-Eastern excavation commenced. In that same year the daughter of Marcelino de Sautuola walked into the dark inner recesses of the Altamira cave and, lifting her lamp, saw frightening paintings on the roof and ran out to her father, who was excavating outside, crying 'Toros! Toros!' – Come and see the bulls. She had found, by accident, the now famous polychromes on the roof at Altamira and the real fact of Upper Palaeolithic art was with us – not, admittedly, accepted as such by the archaeological world for a quarter of a century, and not, perhaps, really a part of the historical perspective of most people until the years following the sensational discovery of Lascaux in 1940 with its widespread popularization in archaeological and general circles.

As people began to study the naturalistic drawings and paintings of Upper Palaeolithic times that were being discovered in the last third of the nineteenth century, and, as they also began to study the prehistoric record in different countries, they became less and less certain that there was a universal common prehistory of man, and that all was evolutionary progress to a common goal of Victorian complacency. The idea of regression was one which both historians and anthropologists had been discussing for some while. The father of British anthropology, as he has been called, Sir E. B. Tylor, when he wrote his *Primitive Culture* in 1871, said that his aim was to 'sketch a theoretical course of civilization among mankind' which he called 'a progression-theory of civilization', but even then he was prepared to admit that 'culture gained by progression may be lost by degradation'. When Dr Arthur Mitchell gave his Rhind Lectures on Archaeology at Edin-

burgh in 1876 and 1878* he was particularly interested in
retrogression and regress. He cited the cities of Copan and
Palenque and particularly the early glory of Egypt. It was, as
Tylor and Mitchell pointed out, the obvious facts of Egyptian
decay which Sir Thomas Browne was commenting on when
he said of her 'she poreth not upon the heavens, astronomy
is died unto her, and knowledge maketh other cycles'. There
it was, in Browne's phrase, and long before Spengler and
Arnold Toynbee were trying to elaborate their historical
cycles with a wealth of learning and tendentious interpretations. To quote Arthur Mitchell's clear words in the seventies:

Within the range of history . . . degradations are found presenting
themselves both in races which are in the states of high and in races
which are in the states of low civilization. In other words savages
become more savage as well as the highly civilized less civilized.
Degradation and development alike occur within the range of history,
and, this being so, can there be any sufficient reason for concluding
that both have not occurred beyond that range?

Prehistory was of course dealing with events beyond the
range of history. It was reasonable, as Mitchell said, to suppose that it, too, had its degradations and devolutions. But was
this merely a reasonable assumption based on an evaluation of
history and a late nineteenth-century scepticism about the
universality of progress? Tennyson, in *Locksley Hall Sixty
Years After*, wrote, in 1886, these oft-quoted lines –

> Evolution ever climbing after some ideal good,
> And Reversion ever dragging Evolution in the mud.

The question was this as regards prehistory: was it thought
that there was degradation and reversion in prehistory just
because it existed in history, and in the philosophical preconceptions of the late Victorians? What one has to ask oneself

---

* Ten of his lectures were reprinted in his book *The Past in the Present; what
is Civilization?* (1880) from which the quotation is taken.

in trying to work out the ideas on prehistory of the late Victorians, and in trying to assess how prehistory affected their ideas if at all, is this: when Gabriel de Mortillet insisted on the picture of technological evolution which prehistory presented, was he making an objective archaeological evaluation which enabled prehistory to confirm the Victorian idea of progress, or was he projecting into prehistory his own widely shared ideas of progress? And, later, was there real archaeological proof of decay and regression in prehistory or was this a late Victorian defeatism projected into the archaeological record?

I regard the discovery of Upper Palaeolithic paintings as of the greatest importance in trying to settle this question, and I need here do little more than touch on the details of the story. In 1864 Lartet and Christy, in a paper in the *Revue archéologique*, showed that Upper Palaeolithic man had mobiliary art – that engraved and carved bones and stones were found in undisturbed deposits in the Dordogne and the Pyrenees. Gradually the fact that these remote men of the Old Stone Age were artists was accepted. But mobiliary (or home) art was one thing: cave art when first discovered was by no means so easily assimilable. We have referred to the discoveries at Altamira. In 1875 Marcelino de Sautuola had discovered black paintings on the back walls of the cave at Altamira, and then and there had claimed them to be of the same age as the deposits in the cave. Four years later his daughter had found the polychromes and in 1880 de Sautuola published the paintings claiming them to be Palaeolithic in age. Meanwhile drawings had been found on the walls of the cave of Chabot in the Ardèche. Altamira and Chabot precipitated a tremendous dispute. Many said that Sautuola was an impostor and a fraud, and that he had hired an artist from Madrid to do the paintings. Others said soldiers with nothing better to do had done them when hiding in the cave. Yet some from the beginning supported the claims of de Sautuola. Among these was Gabriel de

Mortillet who, despite his evolutionary preconceptions, declared: '*C'est l'enfance de l'art, ce n'est pas l'art de l'enfant.*'

In 1895 paintings and engravings were found on the walls of a cave at La Mouthe near Les Eyzies in the Dordogne; the entrance to this cave had been found only after Palaeolithic deposits masking it had been removed. The following year animal drawings were published from the cave of Pair-non-Pair in the Gironde and these were partly covered by undisturbed Palaeolithic deposits. The late Abbé Breuil, for long doyen of experts on the Palaeolithic, but then a young man, realized the significance of the evidence of La Mouthe and Pair-non-Pair on the authenticity of cave art and set it out in an article in 1901 in the *Revue scientifique*. In the same year the now world-famous caves of Les Combarelles and Font de Gaume were discovered near Les Eyzies; in the following year all these discoveries were discussed at the Montauban meeting of the *Association française pour l'avancement des sciences*. A party visited La Mouthe, Les Combarelles, and Font de Gaume and were convinced. Emile Cartailhac, who was at that time the doyen of prehistoric archaeology in France, published an article in *L'Anthropologie* entitled 'Mea culpa d'un sceptique', in which he recanted his earlier disbelief and accepted Upper Palaeolithic art. From the end of Victorian days Upper Palaeolithic art was part of the perspective of prehistory (Plate 3).

The length of time which it took cave art to be accepted by scholars – I do not here refer to the much slower apprehension of it by the general public – was due to the Victorian conception of progress and of similar development. For there were two things that were soon understood about the remarkable flowering of art during a period of the human past which we would now date from say 35,000 to 10,000 B.C. One is that its range in space is restricted to southern France and northern Spain, or so it seemed in the last quarter of the nineteenth century – we know now that examples of it occur in Italy and

Sicily, but even so it is still very restricted. And the second is that it came to an end; the fine naturalism, the exuberant virility, the bright colours, the Disney-like humour of these most ancient paintings and engravings belonged to a style which came to an end. Art did not again reach a comparable level of aesthetic performance in western and west Mediterranean Europe for thousands of years – indeed did not exist at all for thousands of years.

Here was a blow to any idea of prehistory which made the archaeological record the same everywhere, and assumed that there was progress everywhere on parallel lines. It was obvious that, even if everyone in prehistoric Europe had passed through successive stages of stone, bronze, and iron, they had not all possessed artistic ability like those men who had worked at La Mouthe and Altamira and Font de Gaume. Prehistory had to absorb the idea, now perhaps a commonplace to us, of the regional flowering of cultures and to realize that there were cultures, civilizations, societies – call them what you will – in prehistory with different distributions in time and space. It was soon obvious to prehistorians that everyone did not pass through a stage when he painted charging bulls on the roofs of caves, or made great collective tombs of huge megalithic stones, or built multi-ramparted hill forts like Maiden Castle. Prehistory was now becoming a record of cultural achievement set out in parallel columns and not in one evolutionary sequence. XII Maturing adulthood,

That was the lesson which, very gradually, the prehistorians of the Victorian period were learning though it was not generally learnt until the first two decades of the twentieth century. Yet this lesson, if imperfectly, or rather not universally, learnt in late Victorian times, did beg the same old question of cultural origins which we have seen was being asked before. If man did not develop in prehistoric times in a natural and uniform cultural evolution, how then did cultural changes and differences come about?

The interesting thing is that this issue had really already been well discussed by the Scandinavian pioneers of the Three Age system, particularly by Thomsen and Worsaae. It is always necessary to emphasize that the concept of the Three Ages as set out in the writings and teaching and museum practice of Thomsen and Worsaae is not primarily an evolutionary one. They did not regard the Three Ages as forming a 'natural' succession in Denmark. Far from it. In his books Worsaae on many occasions explains that the Bronze Age in Denmark did not develop step by step out of the Danish Stone Age; 'the transition is so abrupt', he wrote in the book translated into English as *The Primeval Antiquities of Denmark* (1849), 'that the bronze period must have commenced with the irruption of a new race of people, possessing a higher degree of cultivation than the earlier inhabitants'. In the same way, he thought, the Iron Age in Denmark was the result of another invasion. The early nineteenth-century Scandinavian archaeologists thus realized clearly that the development of cultural change in prehistory was not by innate organic or super-organic evolution but by the arrival of new ideas from outside – in a word, by diffusion. They even used the word diffusion. 'The universal diffusion of metals could only take place by degrees,' wrote Worsaae. So, from the second quarter of the nineteenth century, we had set out the basic essential idea of the difference in time between the cultures of differing areas. The question now was: how did these new ideas come into an area like Scandinavia – by trade, by the arrival of a small group of people, by invasion, or just by cultural borrowing? And whence?

In his *Prehistoric Times*, Lubbock argued how a Bronze Age could have come into existence in northern Europe and set out the five possibilities which were being discussed in the sixties. First that it was due to Roman influence, secondly to the Etruscans, thirdly to the Phoenicians, fourthly to a new and more civilized people of Indo-European 'race' coming from the east who brought with them a knowledge of bronze and overran Europe dispossessing the earlier Neolithic settlers. The fifth theory, which Lubbock immediately discounted, was the evolutionary one; namely the belief that the earlier inhabitants developed peacefully and gradually on their own into a Bronze Age.

Gradually, the ideas of migrating hordes became popular among late Victorian archaeologists who were reacting from the unilinear idea of progress and realizing that cultural change had to be explained in terms of influence from outside. This problem of interpretation was not confined to the prehistory of northern and western Europe. Schliemann's discovery of the civilization of Mycenae posed the question of the origins of the Mycenaeans. To some they were Aryans from the north, to others, Phoenicians, to others, Carians. The Bronze Age origins in Denmark and the origins of Mycenae were all part of the same general problem of cultural origins. Some insisted on a native element in European prehistory: Salomon Reinach was one of these and he castigated those who constantly sought for invaders from the east in his *Le Mirage oriental* (1893). The great Swedish archaeologist Oscar Montelius, on the other hand, was all for eastern and outside influences and invasions. He strongly argued the *ex oriente lux* theory, especially in his *Orient und Europa* (1899).

At a time when the peoples of Europe were, so to speak, without any civilization whatsoever [he declared], the Orient and particularly the Euphrates region and the Nile were already in enjoyment of a flourishing culture. The civilization which gradually dawned on our continent was for long only a pale reflection of Oriental culture.

Here, then, was an indication of the long way some archaeologists had travelled since the time of the simple unilinear evolutionists. The travel was in the direction which ultimately led to the hyperdiffusionist excesses of Elliot Smith, Perry, and Lord Raglan that we shall discuss later in this course of lectures, and which we shall see are very near to the desires of so many people for a simple explanation of archaeology and history. The Victorians never thought up anything as all-embracing as the Givers of Life of the Heliolithic Civilization of Perry and Elliot Smith, and they had not yet heard of the Sumerians whom Lord Raglan sees as the master-civilizers of the world; but they did not do too badly with their Aryan hordes. Basically they sought a simple all-embracing solution to the problem of human origins. If this solution could not be one of unilateral evolution, why not, then, a few clear-cut and recognizable invasions?

Even in Rice Holmes's *Ancient Britain and the Invasions of Julius Caesar*, published in 1907, our prehistory is set out in terms of a Palaeolithic succeeded by a Neolithic invasion, then by a Bronze Age invasion, and then an Early Iron Age invasion. All this, in the first decade of the twentieth century, was not very far removed from Worsaae. The truth is that by the end of the nineteenth century prehistoric archaeology needed a fresh impetus, a fresh jerk forward with new techniques of discovery, excavation, and interpretation. The late nineteenth-century prehistorians were really only elaborating the basic concepts which had been hammered out before 1859, and as one looks through the successive seven editions of Lubbock's *Prehistoric Times* produced between 1865 and 1913 it is surprising how little change there really was: and I mean here change in fundamental outlook – there was of course plenty of change in detail and many new discoveries to report.

Indeed one senses in the late nineteenth century a feeling that is attacking many prehistorians at the present day, a feeling of the inadequacy of the archaeological record in giving us a full picture of the prehistoric past. It is perhaps a reflection of this feeling that enabled a virtually non-archaeological prehistory to grow up during the nineteenth century, and it is with this non-archaeological prehistory that I wish to concern

myself now. It was incidentally something that had considerable effect on political thought in the twentieth century.

One might say that this non-archaeological prehistory began
in the writings of the humanists of the middle and late eighteenth century, such as the Scottish primitivists who were
interested, in Mr McQuedy's words, 'in the infancy of society',
in Lord Monboddo's views on the origin and progress of
language, in Governor Pownall's notions of Woodland Men
and Land Workers. We find similar views in the writings of
Sven Nilsson, Professor of Zoology at Lund. His views were
originally published in Swedish in 1834 and can be most easily
consulted in their translation into English which appeared in
1868. The translator was Lubbock and the English title *The
Primitive Inhabitants of Scandinavia*.

Nilsson, by the comparative study of existing peoples,
arrived at a classification of prehistoric man based on the mode
of subsistence. There were four stages in his classification,
first the *savage state* – the childhood of the race – when man is
a hunter, fisher, and collector of berries and fruits, and you
must not think I am going back to Governor Pownall when
I remind you that savages are the wild men of the woods –
homines sylvestres. The second stage, according to Nilsson, was
the *herdsman* or *nomad* stage, when hunting was an occasional
occupation but man subsisted essentially on the products of
his herds. The third stage was the *agricultural* – man the agri-
culturist – and the fourth and final stage was *civilization*.
Nilsson defined this on the basis of coined money, writing,
and the division of labour. Now it is not only the professional
archaeologists who had these notions of the development of
society in prehistory but also the general literary world. In
1836 we find Coleridge writing that 'the progress from
savagery to civilization is evidently first from the hunting to
the pastoral stage'.

When Sir Edward Tylor was writing his standard works on
anthropology, he fully recognized the Danish system of the

Three Ages and fully agreed that the Stone Age was the beginning of man's prehistoric development, but he proposed to distinguish three different stages in the human past and these he labelled Savagery, Barbarism, and Civilization. In his *Anthropology; An Introduction to the Study of Man and Civilization*, which was first published in 1881, Tylor defined what he meant by barbarism; it was a state of culture beginning with agriculture, and ending with civilization which by definition meant writing.

These terms and the use of a non-archaeological prehistory of man were developed by the American anthropologist Lewis H. Morgan in his *Ancient Society* (1877). The subtitle of Morgan's work is particularly interesting: it was *Researches in the Lines of Human Progress from Savagery through Barbarism to Civilization*. Tylor had distinguished three stages; Morgan distinguished seven – seven ethnic periods as he called them, as follows: Lower Savagery from the emergence of man to the discovery of fire; Middle Savagery from the discovery of fire to the discovery of the bow and arrow; Upper Savagery from the bow and arrow to pottery; Lower Barbarism from the discovery of pottery to the domestication of animals; Middle Barbarism from the domestication of animals to the smelting of iron ore (at least in the Old World, Morgan had slightly different criteria for these periods in the Americas); Upper Barbarism from the discovery of iron to the invention of a phonetic alphabet; while his seventh and last stage from writing and the alphabet onwards was civilization. Morgan distinguished several civilizations, the ancient civilizations of Egypt, south-west Asia, and the classical lands of Greece and Rome, and then modern civilization of which he himself was a part.

There are two things to remember about Morgan and his schemes. He was himself a unilateral evolutionist and was working out a progressive sequence of man's cultural evolution. He also firmly believed that this sequence developed naturally in different regions. It is not strange that he, an American, should be so convinced of parallel natural cultural evolution. The expeditions of John Lloyd Stephens and Frederick Catherwood in Yucatan in 1839 and 1840 had discovered the lost Mayan cities of Copan, Palenque, Uxmal, and Chichen Itza and had precipitated anew the old issue of diffusion versus independent evolution. For a century and more since the publication of Stephens's *Incidents of Travel in Central America, Chipas and Yucatan* in 1841, the world has been arguing about the origin of Middle American civilization. Diffusion from the Old World, or diffusion from the mythical continents of Atlantis, Lemuria, and Mu on the one hand; independent evolution on the other. Wells Jakeman has summarized the modern view on the problem of Mayan origins:

> The evolution of the Mayan civilization in apparently complete independence of the great culture-complexes of the Old World suggests that its separate historical reconstruction may reveal confirmatory parallels for fixing the chief causes underlying the rise and fall of nations, and for determining the laws of human progress.[*]

While many Old World prehistorians in the twentieth century have not accepted this view, or the relevance of the American cultural record to the interpretation of Old World prehistory, it is not surprising that Lewis Morgan, with the jungle- covered Mayan cities at least nearer his doorstep than they were to the doorsteps of European archaeologists, should have felt that after all, there might be in human history a natural and inevitable cultural evolution that led perhaps separately in Egypt, China, and Middle America to a civilization of literate cities.

[*] Max Wells Jakeman, *The Origin and History of the Mayas*, 1945, p. 17.

CHAPTER FOUR

THE DEVELOPMENT OF MODERN PREHISTORY

In the last lecture, an attempt was made, briefly and, I have no doubt, imperfectly, to give some notion of the idea of prehistory which the late Victorians had and to describe the notions of prehistory which were current between 1859, the *annus mirabilis* which saw the publication of the *Origin of Species* and the public acceptance of the great antiquity of man, and 1913 when the seventh and last edition of Lubbock's *Prehistoric Times* was brought out, a few months after the death of its distinguished author who had invented the terms Palaeolithic and Neolithic (as well as Bank Holidays). I hope I managed to convey that throughout that formative half-century there was not a single and all-pervasive idea of prehistory among the scholars who were, for the first time, seeing prehistory as something that could be obtained by archaeological means. On the contrary there was a great deal of change of thought. At first, in the full flush of Victorian evolutionary thought it seemed that prehistory was just proving the earlier stages of that long single pattern that led from the beginnings of man through to Victorian prosperity itself, 'the heir of all the ages in the foremost files of time', as Tennyson himself described it. But then doubts arose, several development sequences were distinguished, and the phenomena of retrogression and decay were all too apparent if one examined such disturbing things as post-Roman Britain or the end of Upper Palaeolithic art, or the civilization of the Mayas. Indeed anthropologists seemed to be turning away from archaeological prehistory and seeking the keys to the prehistoric past in the comparative study of primitive societies.

There were perhaps, however, two things about which everyone was agreed by the first decade of the twentieth century, as far as prehistoric archaeology was concerned. One was the enormous antiquity of man; that had at last become an essential of historical and anthropological thinking, and the Ussher chronology and the flood had gone for ever, except in the fundamentalist tenets of narrow sects and crank religions. Secondly, no one had any doubt, whatever value or interpretation he gave to the facts of prehistoric archaeology, that in the rise of prehistory there had come about a new discipline of great value and importance. It is perhaps strange, this being so, that prehistory has taken so long to penetrate properly into our universities, and into our awareness and our perspective of the past. That this was so in the last quarter of the nineteenth century no one can have any doubt who reads books, lectures, and papers of that period. I have already quoted what W. E. Gladstone said; in 1871 in his *Primitive Culture* Sir Edward Tylor wrote: 'The history and prehistory of man take their proper places in the general scheme of knowledge', and three years later, in the preface to his *Cave-Hunting* published the year before Mr Gladstone declared he was beginning to see through a dense mist to 'real places, real men, real facts', Professor Boyd Dawkins said triumphantly that 'archaeology, by the use of strictly inductive methods, has grown from a mere antiquarian speculation into a science'.

That was seventy-five years ago at least. In 1874 Boyd Dawkins was congratulating himself and the world in general that archaeology had become a science. Yet if one asks any modern undergraduate to write an essay on the main changes in prehistoric archaeology in the last twenty-five years he will certainly put very high the fact that it has 'recently' become scientific. And any modern professional archaeologist is always declaiming about the development of scientific archaeology;

this always turns out to be the developments he has witnessed or taken part in during the years immediately before his utterance. To a certain extent, and I am not being cynical here, 'scientific' means, in prehistory, modern and recent and anything that is away from the horrid barrow diggers and muddles of the nineteenth century. Yet this must be the main underlying theme in any account of the development of prehistory between 1900 and the present day – the half-century between the seventh edition of *Prehistoric Times* and the present that we are discussing today – that it was at last becoming modern and scientific and leaving behind for ever the non-archaeological prehistory of antiquarian speculation.

Indeed, how could one avoid feeling, as the great discoveries were being made from the turn of the century onwards, that one was living at a time when the prehistoric past was really becoming known at last through archaeological means. In the year 1900 itself Arthur Evans began work at Knossos and unearthed the civilization which he named the Minoan. In 1904 Pumpelly and Schmidt were digging at Anau and the world was learning what a wealth of prehistoric story lay buried in the *tells* and *kurgans* of the Near East – or the Near East as it was to archaeologists and the general public before the curious naming of military commands made it the Middle East.* In 1906 Winckler began work at Boghazkeui, the old capital of the ancient Hittites. In 1918 Campbell Thompson and Hall were working at Ur and Eridu and the Sumerians – postulated as early as 1869 by Oppert, and a reality when de Sarzec began work at Lagash – were at last a common fact of prehistory, a fact which became a dramatic and permanent reality to the world at large when Leonard Woolley excavated the Royal Tombs at Ur in 1926. Anderson, five years before this, had discovered Yang Shao Tsun and established the early stages of Chinese prehistory, and in the same year Sahni had

---

* At least for the British. It is still the Near East to Americans and continental Europeans.

begun work in Harappa and Banerji at Mohenjo-Daro. The next year Sir John Marshall appeared to be bemoaning that it was the misfortune of Indian history that 'its earliest and most obscure pages derive little light from contemporary antiquities'; he had written these words for the first volume of the *Cambridge History of India* before Sahni and Banerji had begun their work. In 1923 in the *Illustrated London News*, Marshall was announcing that the excavations at Harappa and Mohenjo-Daro had revealed a new prehistoric civilization, and was comparing their discovery with Schliemann's discoveries at Tiryns and Mycenae. In the same year, the same journal, which, since (Sir) Bruce Ingram assumed editorship in 1900 has given a coverage to archaeology which is the envy of the world, was announcing that Howard Carter and Lord Caernarvon had found and excavated the tomb of Tutankhamen.

These were indeed years of heroic discovery – the quarter-century from Knossos to Tutankhamen, from Anau to the Royal Tombs at Ur – and it is amazing, looking back on them, that four were taken up with the first great world war, with its senseless cessation of archaeological activities and its tragic slaughter of potential and real archaeologists. These twenty-five years were also a period of amazing change in the methods and aims of prehistory. Indeed it is no exaggeration to say that a revolution took place in prehistoric archaeology during this quarter century and if I were pinned in a corner and asked what were really the formative years of prehistory I would say that there were two periods, the first from 1807 to 1859 – the half-century between Thomsen and the *annus mirabilis*, and the second from 1900 to 1925 – the quarter-century in our own country between Pitt-Rivers and the men who in the early twenties revolutionized British prehistory. For there was a great revolution in prehistory in the first quarter of the present century, and it is a revolution which is most clearly seen in the northern countries of Europe and particularly in the British Isles. Indeed it is not extravagant to refer to it as the

British revolution in prehistory, just as the great changes that produced the Three Age system in the first quarter of the nineteenth century were a Danish (or Scandinavian) revolution in prehistory.

This 'revolution' which I have dramatically but not sensationally called it, was a series of remarkable changes which had actually started before 1900. The sum total of these changes in retrospect, adds up to revolutionary change: 1900 was the year in which General Pitt-Rivers died, and these changes of which we are now speaking began with his own archaeological work. This remarkable man was born Lane-Fox and took the name of Pitt-Rivers when, in 1880, he inherited the Rivers estates, over 29,000 acres of land, including much of Cranborne Chase. Before this, as a professional soldier, he had been concerned with the use and development of the rifle between 1851 and 1857 at Woolwich, Enfield, Malta, and Hythe; he was virtually the creator of the Hythe School of Musketry. He studied the development of firearms and as he did so he found himself arranging collections of types in developing sequences. Himself imbued with the Darwinian notions of evolution, and constantly examining the sequences of firearms and noting their differences, he formulated the idea that all archaeological material, that is to say all the material remains of the past, could be arranged in sequences – in what the archaeologist and anthropologist now call typological sequences.

The idea of typology was not something invented by Pitt-Rivers; it had existed in the work of the early Danish and Swedish archaeologists, and at the same time as Pitt-Rivers was working out his sequences, a man like John Evans was busily classifying and arranging in sequences bronze and stone tools. The collection of tools and weapons which Pitt-Rivers was making soon outgrew his house, and they eventually found their way to Oxford where a special annex of the University Museum was built to house them.

The Pitt-Rivers collections were arranged not geographically but typologically, and they did not necessarily contain remarkable or beautiful things. He said himself that his collections were

not for the purpose of surprising anyone, either by the beauty or value of the objects exhibited, but solely with a view to instruction. For this purpose ordinary and typical specimens rather than rare objects have been selected and arranged in sequence.

And in the lectures he gave in London between 1867 and 1874, he kept stressing the need for the study of all material objects of human culture. One of the mainsprings of an interest in antiquarian matters in the seventeenth and eighteenth centuries was the cultivation of taste, the collection and cultivation of the beautiful object which could adorn the cabinet and give intrinsic pleasure as well as, or indeed instead of, being merely a historical document. Gradually, as the nineteenth century had transformed antiquarianism into archaeology, taste, and the contemplation of beautiful things were disappearing. As Dr Joan Evans has said recently, with a tinge of regret with which we can all sympathize, it was Pitt-Rivers who gave the death blow to taste. He finally exorcised taste from archaeology.*

Of course, one man by himself does not necessarily do these things. He appears to us, looking back at him, as a symbol of change. Flinders Petrie was as much an agent of this change as Pitt-Rivers; his too was an important influence in the exorcising of the ghost of taste. He began his work in Egypt in 1881 and was soon formulating what became the new method in prehistoric archaeology. He insisted on the collection and description of everything found and this was emphasized in his *Methods and Aims in Archaeology* published in 1904. Petrie began excavating in Egypt a year after Lane-Fox had become Pitt-Rivers and assumed control of his large estates. Pitt-

* Joan Evans, *A History of the Society of Antiquaries*, London, 1956, p. 341.

Rivers at once began a series of excavations in Wessex; he had dug before and some of his techniques stem back to Canon Greenwell and William Cunnington. But whatever he had learnt from past excavators, he developed and perfected. He had plenty of money and plenty of time, and a long training in military staff methods, survey, and precision behind him. His excavations were well organized, thoroughly carried out; he demanded the highest standards of care from his men. He insisted on the total excavation of sites and substituted this for the old-time technique of digging hopefully during an afternoon into a barrow and looking for a primary burial with a beaker or urn or bronze dagger that would look nice in one's private collection. And he began excavating settlement sites as well as burial mounds.

Pitt-Rivers also insisted on the accurate recording of his excavations and that this record should contain the exact position where everything was found. He made plans and sections, detailed drawings, and descriptions of all his excavations, and even made models of the main sites which he dug. There is no doubt that the modern techniques of excavation now practised in north-western Europe began in his work on Cranborne Chase between 1880 and 1900, and the four privately printed volumes describing his work achieved a very high standard of archaeological publication. As I have said elsewhere, 'in fifteen years he transformed excavation from the pleasant hobby of barrow digging to an arduous scientific pursuit'.* And throughout he insisted on the study of ordinary objects and of *all* ordinary objects. 'Common things are of more importance than particular things, because they are more prevalent,' he wrote in 1898.

Here then, right at the turn of the century, was the beginning of a revolution in archaeological technique. Typology, the meticulous examination of sites, the study of the totality of phenomena – these were the things which Pitt-Rivers and

* G. E. Daniel, *A Hundred Years of Archaeology*, 1950, p. 173.

Petrie bequeathed as an archaeological legacy to the early
twentieth century. Petrie himself went on to practise these
techniques until the forties. It was however a legacy which was
not extensively taken up, developed, and expanded until after
the 1914–18 war, and it was developed in Britain mainly by
two men, R. E. M. Wheeler and Cyril Fox. In his autobiography, *Still Digging* (1955), Sir Mortimer Wheeler has
looked back at the moment in 1919 when he began his serious
career of excavation.

> Between 1880 and 1900 [he wrote], General Pitt-Rivers in Cran-
> borne Chase had brought archaeological digging and recording to a
> remarkable degree of perfection, and had presented his methods and re-
> sults meticulously in several imposing volumes. Then what? Nothing.
> Nobody paid the slightest attention to the old man. One of his
> assistants had even proceeded to dig up a lake-village much as Schlie-
> mann had dug up Troy, or St John Hope, Silchester; like potatoes.
> Not only had the clock not gone on, but it had been set back.*

This is Wheeler's crisp verdict. Admittedly the war of
1914–18 carried away many potential archaeologists. Wheeler
himself describes how he was the only one of four university
students digging at Wroxeter in 1913 to survive the war, and
the sense of isolation which was so apparent to him in 1919.
The earlier tradition was carried on to some extent between
Pitt-Rivers's death and Wheeler's work at Segontium in 1921
by a few workers such as J. P. Bushe Fox in Wroxeter and
Hengistbury Head, James Curle at Newstead in Scotland, and
John Ward in South Wales, as Wheeler himself has recognized.
Nevertheless the work of Wheeler and Fox in the early twenties
had the real appearance of a fresh start; they turned back to the
Pitt-Rivers traditions, expanded and improved them, and so
changed, handed them on to the excavators of the present day.
It is not my object here to catalogue the excavations by which
Wheeler established his reputation and perfected his technique,
but even those of you who do not know of the beginnings at

* Sir Mortimer Wheeler, *Still Digging*, 1955, pp. 66–7.

Segontium and the Brecon Gaer and at Caerleon will know of his excavations at Maiden Castle before the 1939–45 war, at Harappa, Arikamedu, and Taxila in India, towards the end and after the war, and more recently at Stanwick. Nor is it my object to do more than mention in passing those who have carried on the traditions of British excavation re-created by Fox and Wheeler in the twenties – men like Ian Richmond, Christopher Hawkes, Grahame Clark, Stuart Piggott, C. A. Ralegh Radford, C. W. Phillips, to mention a few living names of those who are at the top of their profession; or men like V. Nash Williams, B. H. St J. O'Neil, and Sean Ó Ríordáin, to mention a few who, alas, have died in the fullness of their work. Nor do I want to create the impression, because I am emphasizing the British aspects of this story, that the same changes were not taking place in some other parts of northern Europe – in Holland, Germany, and Scandinavia. It was not, however, happening all over Europe, and we may reflect with pride that the British tradition was a very important element in the re-creation of a new archaeological field technique.

We have then a new factor in the ideas of prehistory which have been formulated in the last fifty years; the idea that prehistory should not merely be written from archaeological sources but that it should be based on archaeological information which is accurate, detailed, and complete. While the early nineteenth-century excavations were, if not treasure hunts, but very partial examinations of the material, our modern excavations – or at least the best of them – are total and complete examinations of the material. I would remind you here that there are two aspects of excavation: there is the actual surgery of the landscape by pick, shovel, trowel, knife, and scalpel with all the photographic and diagrammatic recording of this operation, and there is then the examination of everything found by every available method – the analysis of form and material of all the artifacts found, and of all associated material. This analytical aspect of the study of the archaeological material has been one of the major developments since the early twenties and now we are accustomed to have in archaeological reports the findings of specialists who have worked on pollens or on snails, on soils, or on grain impressions. Even more exciting has been the development since 1945 of the technique of exact dating by Carbon-14 analysis. This remarkable technique, first discovered by Libby at Chicago as a by-product of research into atomic physics, enables organic substances to be dated in calendar years by the quantity of Carbon-14 they contain. This is a very bad and bald and brief way of describing this amazing technique which has enabled people to date the late Mesolithic settlement at Seamer, to 7500 B.C., and Upper Palaeolithic art to between 30,000 and 10,000 B.C.

This is certainly one of the things that one must stress in try-ing to see what is really represented by the modern scientific technique of excavation – it is the extraction of every available piece of evidence that can be used for building up the historical contexts of the past, and for that matter even the detailed re-cording of evidence which in itself at the time does not seem to make sense. It is one of the many remarkable features, for example, of Pitt-Rivers's work that in his notes, excavation reports, and models, he recorded information about his exca-vations which could be used later, and indeed has been used later, by men like Professor Hawkes, to arrive at conclusions which Pitt-Rivers did not or could not have reached.* It is often said that all excavation is not only a recovery of the past but to a certain degree a destruction of the past, and in many ways this is true. Everyone who undertakes the surgery of the landscape – which is excavation – has a responsibility to future generations of archaeologists and historians as well as to his own generation. This responsibility is discharged not only by complete and meticulous digging but by complete and metic-ulous record. It is one of the features of present mid-twentieth-

* C. F. C. Hawkes, *Archaeological Journal*, 1954, p. 145.

century excavation which vitally affects what ideas we now have of the prehistoric past that we live in a climate of thought which believes in the highest possible standards of excavational technique and publication.

I have mentioned Sir Cyril Fox as one of those who in the early twenties did so much to re-create in Britain the technique of excavation which Pitt-Rivers had first created. Fox was also a field archaeologist of the first rank. There is often confusion among archaeologists as to what is meant by field archaeology; Sir Leonard Woolley once reviewed O. G. S. Crawford's book, *Archaeology in the Field*, and declared with surprise that he had always thought of himself as a field archaeologist until he read Crawford's book and found that he was 'only an excavator!' In the minds of many people there is a dichotomy between the indoors or study or closet archaeologist, and the archaeologist who goes out into the field – the dirt archaeologist as he is sometimes called, the man who gets mud on his boots and sand in his eyes. But the activities of the archaeologist in the field are of two different kinds: first, excavation which is the surgical aspect of field archaeology, and secondly the non-surgical or physical aspect of the study of the visible material remains of the past. It is this second aspect to which Crawford was referring when he used the phrase field archaeology as distinct from excavation; this tradition of field archaeology is one which has been built up in Britain over the centuries. It began with exact observers and painstaking travellers to the past like John Aubrey and Edward Lhuyd, and was developed in the late nineteenth century and early twentieth century by men like Williams Freeman whose *Field Archaeology as illustrated by Hampshire* was published in 1915.

Crawford and Fox were heirs of this field archaeological tradition, and developed it in various ways, the tradition which produced on the one hand *The Long Barrows of the Cotswolds*, and the megalithic and period maps of the Ordnance Survey, and, on the other, *The Archaeology of the*

Cambridge Region, and *Offa's Dyke*. This aspect of modern field archaeology has a feature closely akin to what we have been saying about excavational technique. It, too, aims at total information, at the study of the totality of visible archaeological phenomena. When John Aubrey was asked to write about Avebury and Stonehenge he begged to be allowed to defer his work until he had seen all the other comparable monuments in England and Wales. Because of the extension of this idea not only in principle but in practice, we can now study all the representatives of any archaeological category of monument or artifact. If, for example, at the present moment we want to study Stonehenge and Avebury and say, as John Aubrey did, that we can do so only against the background of all other comparable examples of stone circles, we can do so, because twentieth-century field archaeology has brought us to the position where we can view the total pattern of these monuments. The distribution map is one of the main instruments of archaeological research and exposition, but because it is a commonplace of books and papers, do not let us forget what it is trying to do – to accomplish and to demonstrate the totality of information about some archaeological fact, to study the total evidence in space regarding one aspect of the material remains of the past.

I have said that the field archaeologist is concerned with the visible material remains of the past and so he is and was. He is essentially one who plods laboriously over the surface of the ground observing barrows and linear earthworks and the low grass-covered banks of long-ruined houses or deserted fields. Williams Freeman, over half a century ago, noted that by the long shadows of a late summer evening a field archaeologist on a hill could see earthworks with a clarity denied him when standing on them; they fell into patterns not visible on the ground. He once said to Crawford that 'one ought to be a bird to be a field archaeologist'. The development of aircraft and of aerial photography during and after the 1914–18 war enabled archaeologists virtually to become birds (Plate 4). After that war these opportunities were brilliantly seized by no one so well as O. G. S. Crawford in England. But air photography not only revealed what Williams Freeman expected the air archaeologist to observe, namely shadow marks, but crops and soil marks leading in a dramatic way to the discovery of sites, in apparently flat fields, that were totally invisible to the ground observer. I know of few things more dramatic in archaeological technique than walking over a ploughed field in spring armed with an air photograph showing the marks of ploughed-out banks and filled-in ditches on a photograph taken in the height of the growth of the previous June's corn, and being totally unable to see on the ground these buried ghosts of a prehistoric landscape. Aerial reconnaissance, like the technique of Carbon-14 dating, is one of the most remarkable and surprising advances in the archaeologist's technique in the last quarter-century or more.

But what, you may ask, do all these technical advances add up to – these scientific techniques, this total excavation, our new typologies, our total field surveys, the distribution maps, and air photography? First and foremost they add up, with all the fresh discoveries that are being made, to an enormous body of facts, and what is more, an enormously complicated body of facts. Nowhere was and is this more directly apparent than in the study of cultural sequences. We have seen that the sequence of cultures became more and more complicated as the detailed knowledge of archaeology developed. And what is more, the sequences appeared to be different in different areas. What was even more complicated was that the old idea of a sequence in a single area was collapsing. A man like de Mortillet had organized an elaborate scheme for French archaeology whose basic feature was successive periods or epochs. If we look at Gabriel de Mortillet's *Formation de la nation française* published in 1897, we get at once a clear idea of the single sequence idea. Here the prehistoric past of man is divided into three ages of Stone, Bronze, and Iron, and these are split up into *périodes*, namely the Stone Age into *éolithique*, *paléolithique*, and *néolithique*, and the Iron Age, for example, into *galatienne* (the Galatians to whom St Paul addressed an Epistle were, some of us forget, Celts), the *romaine*, and the *mérovingienne*. These *périodes* were in turn split up into *époques*; there is no point in detailing them here, but let us just look at the division of the Palaeolithic. This was split up into six *époques*, namely the Chellean, Acheulian, Mousterian, Solutrean, Magdalenian, and Tourassian. It did look, even if the prehistoric sequences were not the same in neighbouring countries, as though the story was merely one of detailing the epochs.

In the beginning of the twentieth century the whole idea of these successive epochs began to be doubted and the fabric of subdivisions to crumble. In 1909 at the Grotte de Valle, near Gibaja (Santander) in north Spain, the Abbé Breuil and Professor Obermaier discovered a classic deposit of one 'epoch', namely the Azilian, together with microlithic flints typical of another 'epoch', the Tardenoisian. After this, archaeologists who had been arguing whether the Azilian came before or after the Tardenoisian could stop arguing. 'After this discovery,' said Hugo Obermaier, 'it could no longer be questioned that the Azilian and the Tardenoisian were contemporary.' But what did it mean if two epochs were going to be contemporary? It meant of course that they were not epochs, that the archaeologists, who, after all, had developed out of being geologists and had for long been thinking in geological terms of time and fossil-directors, had to rethink their basic principles and think in terms of historical time and man.

All this was really the great moment when prehistoric archaeology broke away from the quite understandably inherited conceptions of geology and the natural sciences. The human geographers and anthropologists had for some while been canvassing a new idea with regard to human groupings, and an idea which was to supersede the political idea of nations and tribes. Ratzel in Germany in the eighties of the nineteenth century had been distinguishing what he called 'cultural complexes', and his pupil Leo Frobenius developed this idea and studied what he called 'culture-circles'. German ethnologists like Graebner, Schmidt, Ankermann, and others gradually extended this idea and soon archaeologists began to see that what they were studying was not a series of epochs but an assemblage of cultures. The prehistorian had been studying the distribution of prehistoric life in time and space; if these distributions and their associations were planned on a graph with space–time coordinates, it was found that lenticular-shaped masses developed and to these masses – which are persistent assemblages of material traits – the prehistorian now gave the name 'culture'. This is perhaps an unfortunate use of a more widespread term, and it is an especially limited form of a much wider concept; but at least from the early years of the nineteenth century through to the 1939–45 war, it seemed a good and a workable concept. The prehistorian had then to readjust his views, and to realize that he was no longer dealing with unilateral sequences but that he was studying the distribution in time and space of the culture (and of necessity mainly the material culture) of different societies.

This new idea took a long time to penetrate into the views of teachers and workers who were imbued with the nineteenth-century ideas of unilateral sequences to such an extent as almost to have given it a religious significance. Perhaps religious significance is the right word to use here. The earlier sequence of Flood and 4004 B.C. had been exchanged for a sequence of epochs, and to many people in the earlier twenties of this century, this new sequence had attained something of the status of an archaeological fundamentalist doctrine. Compare George Grant MacCurdy's table: 'The Chronology of Prehistory' in his admirable book *Human Origins: A Manual of Prehistory* published in 1924, or Macalister's *Textbook of*

European Archaeology (1921) or M. C. Burkitt's *Prehistory* (also published in 1921) with Gordon Childe's *Dawn of European Civilization* the first edition of which came out in 1925. I have described Childe's *Dawn* as 'not merely a book of incomparable archaeological erudition but . . . a new starting-point for prehistoric archaeology'.* These words were written ten years ago and I would not now want to modify them in any way. Here, in 1925, with the *Dawn* was a new starting-point in prehistory. Gone was the simple evolutionary cultural sequence. Here was a prehistory studying the complexity of cultures, studying human society in the prehistoric past. Childe's lead was soon followed all over the world by those analysing and writing about prehistory. One might say that one of the main tasks of the archaeological synthesist in the fifteen to twenty years following 1925 seemed to be the elaboration of individual cultures; and for the simple evolutionary sequence we begin to get, instead, Beaker Cultures, Food-vessel Cultures, Passage-grave Cultures, Rinyo–Clacton Cultures, and when suitable geographical or taxonomic names ran out, we reverted to letters and numbers and there appeared Neolithic A and B, and Iron Age A, B, and C.

The British Isles themselves provide an admirable example of this process at work. In the times of the earlier synthesists, it was all very easy to understand and to write about. I have already referred to Rice Holmes and his *Ancient Britain and the Invasions of Julius Caesar*: there in the simple synthesis of 1907 the Neolithic race or people introduced the Neolithic, they were replaced by the Bronze Age race or people who brought in metal-working, and eventually by the Iron Age race who introduced the Early Iron Age. But soon there were cracks in this admirably simple structure. Arthur Evans, later to become famous as the discoverer of the Minoan civilization of Crete, published in 1890 in *Archaeologia* his finds of what he described as a Late Celtic urn-field at Aylesford in Kent; he moreover

---

* G. E. Daniel, *A Hundred Years of Archaeology*, p. 247.

identified the Aylesford people with the Belgae who were in history known as invaders of south-east Britain. In doing this he was of course recognizing a separate culture within the Early Iron Age, and a separate group of invaders within the Three-Age invasion pattern of prehistory set out by Rice Holmes and his contemporaries. O. G. S. Crawford working on distributional and other studies suggested, in the early twenties, that the Bronze Age was not a single and unitary phase of development and that the Late Bronze Age was a separate culture introduced by a separate group of invaders.

By the late twenties then, the story of Britain in post-Palaeolithic times was already becoming more complicated than the late nineteenth-century systematists had believed possible. A Neolithic was succeeded by an Early and Middle Bronze Age culture broken by an invasion which brought in the Late Bronze Age, then a further Early Iron Age invasion which itself contained further separate invasions like the Belgic Aylesford invasion of Evans.

In their *Archaeology in England and Wales 1914–31* T. D. Kendrick and C. F. C. Hawkes set out a complicated picture of cultures and invasions. But our best example of the logical evolution of Childe's ideas is provided by Childe himself in his book *The Prehistoric Communities of the British Isles*, first published in 1940. Here there is set out an amazing sequence of cultures – amazing that is to a person brought up on Gabriel de Mortillet or Rice Holmes. If we look at southern England alone we find Windmill Hill and Peterborough Neolithic cultures, the cultures of the Collective Tomb Builders, the Beaker cultures, the Wessex culture, the Food-vessel and Cinerary Urn cultures, the Deverel–Rimbury Late Bronze Age people, then Iron Age A 1, Iron Age A 2, Iron Age B, and the Belgae of Iron Age C. Here was indeed complexity and detail, but, one asks, what was happening to man in all this complexity of detail and culture? Was he being forgotten?

One thing was sure. The old idea of a master race or a

master civilizing people was vanishing. As the records of the past become detailed in such a complicated way in each region studied, it was impossible to see one group of civilizers spreading from one region. Rather could one see no more than small-scale and localized movements, such as the Belgae from north-east France and Belgium to south-east England, or the builders of passage graves from south-west Spain and Portugal to Brittany, Ireland, and west Wales. Prehistory began to look in the thirties and forties as though it would resolve itself into the exercise of tracing small cultural movements and invasions. The great master race had gone, at least in official prehistory, but, as we shall see in the next lecture, it was by no means entirely gone, and I think we shall appreciate that in the hyperdiffusionist theories of Elliot Smith, Perry, and Lord Raglan there is not merely a survival of the old nineteenth-century ideas of master races, not merely a far-reaching conviction that nothing can be invented twice, but a deep-seated desire for a simple story of man's past, and a genuine and not unnatural reaction against the complicated cultural and invasion pattern which was emerging as prehistory in the second quarter of the twentieth century.

The official prehistorians, however, who taught and worked during the period from Childe's *Dawn* in 1925 to the 1939–45 war paid little attention to those who were finding their gradual elaboration of the cultural sequence difficult to master. And we must admit here and now that the detail of prehistory is difficult to assimilate; it is not to be wondered at that the general public sometimes prefer the simplicity of Phoenicians and Druids and Egyptians to Beaker Folk and Iron Age B.

But, on the whole, I think it fair to say that between 1925 and 1939, the period with which we have been concerned, official prehistorians did not bother a very great deal about what the public could make out of prehistory, or whether prehistory was popular with the public. To them the task was, by scientific excavation, by rigorous comparative study, and by the use of all ancillary scientific techniques possible, to get out the record of the past. And this was not a single unitary record, not the record of the spread of a master race, but a record of hundreds of cultures each varying in distribution in time and space.

Prehistory had become a layer cake but a cake whose layers changed as you turned it round and moved to a different part of the world. Then as you turned the cake you saw that the differently coloured layers, gaily stuffed with the artificial material of past human societies, were in fact not layers but lenticles. But the general analogy of a layer cake is a correct one and when I was an undergraduate and research student before the war it did seem that it was a complicated layer cake that I was studying. Do not misunderstand me; I am not trying to make fun out of this essential phase in the development of prehistory. I am only saying that this was in the thirties the prevalent view of prehistory; just as the fog and the flood had been replaced by the unilateral evolutionary sequences of the Victorians, so now, a half-century of new techniques and vastly increased knowledge produced us this gaily coloured layer cake.

We shall see how this layer cake satisfied or dissatisfied those who came to admire and eat it – historians, geographers, anthropologists, politicians, prehistorians themselves. We shall begin by looking at those who deliberately set it aside – the hyperdiffusionists who, by their actions, could almost be said to have set aside also a hundred years and more of archaeology, and gone back to the guesswork of pre-archaeological prehistory.

CHAPTER FIVE

DIFFUSION AND DISTRACTION

WE are, at first, mainly concerned with a very great man who was a Fellow of my own College in Cambridge, and who has been described by Warren Dawson, who edited a book of essays that form the biographical record of his life, as 'one of the foremost anatomists and thinkers of his age', and also as 'one of the outstanding intellectual personalities of his age'. This man, Grafton Elliot Smith, was, and is, the outstanding example of one who fell, as those interested in prehistory are prone to fall, into that extraordinary and interesting intellectual error – the simplistic heresy of hyperdiffusion.

Grafton Elliot Smith was born at Grafton in New South Wales in 1871 – the very year in which Tylor published his *Primitive Culture*. Not only because of this coincidence, nor even because Elliot Smith was himself later to write much about Tylor, we must now take a backward glance at this most distinguished figure, father of British anthropology as he has been called, friend of Huxley, Wallace, Spencer, Lyell, Lubbock, and Darwin, whose work we have already very briefly touched upon. Tylor, whose dates are 1832 to 1917, was, to Elliot Smith, 'one of the most significant figures of the Victorian age', and he says these words in his essay on Tylor in *The Great Victorians* (edited by H. J. Massingham and Hugh Massingham), and declares that he used these words advisedly because Tylor thought 'the most vital thing in the world is the understanding of human nature'.

Tylor travelled because his health broke down when working in his father's brass foundry. He travelled in Mexico with Henry Christy, the English banker who worked with the French palaeontologist Lartet in the exploration of Upper

Palaeolithic sites in the Dordogne. Breakdowns in health have only too often been most detrimental to scholarship: here was one which, together with the stray meeting with Christy, was extremely beneficial to learning. Tylor's interests were turned to anthropology. His first book related to his travels: it was called *Anahuac or Mexico and the Mexicans* (1861). His second was *Researches into the Early History of Mankind*, and it came out in 1865 – the year of the publication of Lubbock's *Prehistoric Times* – and was nothing short of epoch-making. It was, of course, primarily a plea for the study of existing preliterate societies but also for the study of the origins of man.

Civilization [he wrote], being a process of long and complex growth, can only be thoroughly understood when studied throughout its entire range; that the past is continually needed to explain the present, and the whole to explain the past.

In his *Researches* he fully examined the various views about the origins of civilization and of cultural change.

Sometimes [he wrote] it may be ascribed to the like working of men's minds under like conditions, and, sometimes, it is a proof of blood relationship, or of intercourse, direct or indirect, between the races among whom it is found.

Six years later, the year in which, as we have said, Grafton Elliot Smith was born, Tylor elaborated the argument of his earlier book in his *Primitive Culture*, and then, ten years later, in his *Anthropology, an Introduction to the Study of Man and Civilization*. Tylor's subsequent career need not concern us unduly here. In 1883 he became Keeper of the University Museum in Oxford – the Museum which housed the Pitt-Rivers collections: in 1884 he was made Reader in Anthropology and twelve years later became a Professor – the first Professor of Anthropology in the British Isles.

What is important, here and now, is that Tylor was a great

hero to Elliot Smith, and that Tylor himself was a diffusionist.
When I say this I must immediately explain how I am using
this somewhat tendentious word. There were, in the second
half of the nineteenth century, as we have seen, two explanations current as to the origin of the cultural changes which
were manifest in the archaeological record, in history and in
the modern world, and these explanations were usually centred
over such things as the appearance, in two different parts of
the world in the archaeological and ethnographical record, of
apparently the same cultural features. One explanation was
that these features had evolved separately and developed independently. The other was that a feature had spread from
one area to another, that it had in fact been diffused – by
trade, by the movement of people, or by culture contact. It
is these two explanations of culture change that we refer to
when we talk of evolution versus diffusion in the study of
human cultural development.

There is of course no necessary conflict between these two
views; as Lowie said in the twentieth century, looking back
at the Anthropological Institute in the nineteenth century, here
'evolution . . . lay down amicably beside diffusion'. As we
have seen, the early Scandinavian archaeologists believed in
the possible truth of both evolution and diffusion, and so did
Pitt-Rivers. So did Tylor, and you will remember the passage
I have just quoted from Tylor in which he mentioned several
agencies of cultural change – the like working of men's minds,
blood relationship, and intercourse.

The controversy about all this begins when we start to argue
about the relative importance of the factors in cultural change,
and when we find people manoeuvring themselves into, or
pledging, positions in which only one explanation is possible.
Adolf Bastian, the German scholar born in Bremen in 1826,
is the out-and-out evolutionist who would not believe in
diffusion, and a textbook example of such a person. He argued
that by a general law the psychical unity of man everywhere

produced similar ideas; different geographical environments might produce different responses, and there could of course be contacts in later historic times, but the basic idea was the psychic unity of man and, therefore, the independent evolution of culture. These ideas of Bastian's were a form of superorganic or cultural or social evolution. Others interested in anthropology flew to the opposite extreme and one such early diffusionist was a Miss Buckland who, from 1878 onwards, set out in a series of papers – they have names like Primitive Agriculture, Prehistoric Intercourse between East and West, Four as a Sacred Number, etc. – a most violent and uncompromising hyperdiffusionism. According to Miss Buckland – and this is the key doctrine that is implicit in Elliot Smith and his followers – civilization was never, *never* independently acquired. It *could* not be and it *was* not. If you read Miss Buckland it will give you a foretaste of Elliot Smith, for she was writing about sun and serpent worship, and the spread of agriculture, weaving, pottery, and metals all over the earth.*

Miss Buckland was writing her polemics as Grafton Elliot Smith was growing up in New South Wales and qualifying as a doctor at Sydney. It soon became clear to his chief at Sydney, Professor J. T. Wilson, that Elliot Smith was 'meant for a lifework of scientific investigation rather than for the professional life of a medical practitioner'. He was sent to England, became a Research Student at St John's College, Cambridge, in 1896, and a Research Fellow there three years later. In 1900 Alexander Macalister, the Professor of Anatomy in Cambridge, conveyed to the young Elliot Smith an invitation to become the first occupant of the chair of anatomy at the Government Medical School at Cairo. The prime factor in the development of Elliot Smith's hyperdiffusionism was his stay in Egypt, but I think it may well have been Alexander Macalister himself

* For Miss A. W. Buckland see R. H. Lowie, *History of Ethnological Theory*, London, 1937, p. 90 and footnote 10.

who first interested Elliot Smith in the problems and pitfalls of cultural origins. Of Macalister, Elliot Smith wrote:

His chief interest is anthropological. If anything delights him more than inventing some new craniometric index it is the manufacture of some cacophonous name to brand it. But he is equally interested in Egyptian history, in Irish and Gaelic literature and archaeology, in the evolution of Ecclesiastical Vestments ... in the Cambridge collegiate system, in the specific identity of the Egyptian cat, and the progress of the Cambridge Presbyterian Church, among many more or less (probably less) kindred subjects.

This enormous catholicity of interest Elliot Smith admired and practised.

Elliot Smith fell in love with Cairo – 'the gayest and most cosmopolitan city on the face of the earth,' he wrote, 'and intensely fascinating'. The fascination was, of course, partly the antiquities which obtruded themselves on the attention of an intelligent, alert, inquiring traveller like Elliot Smith. 'But,' he wrote in 1901, 'I have not quite resisted the temptation to dabble in Egyptology.'

Not quite. The more's the pity. Soon he was involved in the study of ancient human remains from early Egyptian sites and from predynastic sites. He was able to study a chronologically unbroken series of human remains from 4000 B.C. to 2000 B.C. and then on to Coptic graves. The result of his complete examination was his book _The Ancient Egyptians_ first published in 1911. In 1902 he was referring to 'this sudden burst into anthropology', but the following year was saying, 'for the next six months I expect to be a slave to anthropology', and in that year he made his first detailed study of the technique of mummification – a study which according to Warren Dawson was destined 'to have such far-reaching effects'.

What a true comment this was; mummification was the key-point in Elliot Smith's great Egyptocentric hyperdiffusionist doctrine. He believed that the technique of embalming was so complicated in Egypt that it could not have been invented identically, in all its complexity, anywhere else. Whenever, therefore, he came across the practice of embalming and mummification elsewhere he felt himself forced to conclude that it had spread from Egypt. 'Little did I realize,' he wrote in the preface to the second (1923) edition of his *Ancient Egyptians*, 'when I was writing what was intended to be nothing more than a brief interim report . . . that this little book was destined to open up a new view – or rather to revise and extend an old and neglected method of interpretation of the history of civilization.' Eagerly, he took up the diffusionist view with energy and zeal and with much of the ardour of a missionary.

The details of Elliot Smith's career from Egypt onwards are simple: he went to Manchester as Professor of Anatomy in 1909 and to University College, London, in 1919. He died in 1937. At Manchester and London he proved himself as a great anatomist, teacher, and administrator. In both these places, as well as wherever he travelled over the world, he also preached his doctrines of the diffusion of culture from Egypt. These doctrines were set out in many books. First his *Migrations of Early Culture* in 1915, then *The Evolution of the Dragon* in 1919, *Elephants and Ethnologists* in 1924, *In the Beginning: the origin of Civilization* in 1928, *Human History* in 1930, *The Diffusion of Culture* in 1933, to mention the most important statements of his case in book form. He had many enthusiastic disciples: as for example Wilfred Jackson who in 1917 wrote *Shells as Evidence of the Migrations of Early Culture* and Warren Dawson who wrote *Custom of Couvade* in 1929, but most of all his disciple was W. J. Perry who was first Reader in Comparative Religion in the University of Manchester when Elliot Smith was there, and then Reader of Cultural Anthropology in London when Elliot Smith moved there.

Perry was in many ways more enthusiastic and intransigent than his master. He wrote *The Children of the Sun* (1923), *The Origin of Magic and Religion* (1923), *The Megalithic Culture of*

Indonesia (1918), and a general summary designed for the ordinary reader called *The Growth of Civilization*. This last book was first published in 1924 and was reissued in 1937 by Penguin Books Ltd with all the widespread public appeal and wide circulation that such publication acquires. In the brief description on the jacket of the Penguin Books edition, it was said of Perry: 'He is one of the chief supporters of the "diffusionist" theory of the growth of culture.' In an analysis of the growth of this theory he stresses that two things most affected Elliot Smith: the first, which we have mentioned, was embalming and mummification. The second was megalithic monuments; Elliot Smith had conceived the idea that the pyramids and mastabas of ancient Egypt were the prototypes of the megalithic monuments that are found, in a very wide diversity of form, all over the ancient world. Elliot Smith could not believe that mummification and megalithic architecture could have been invented more than once and he, therefore, concluded that both 'practices' had been diffused from ancient Egypt.

He then began to see most of the elements of all culture as originating in Egypt, and defined a culture-complex of about thirty centuries ago which spread 'like an exotic leaven' – the words are those of Elliot Smith and Perry – over the world taking with it civilization. This original Egyptian civilization was the Heliolithic or Archaic Civilization; Elliot Smith and Perry saw small groups of people setting out, mainly by sea, from Egypt and colonizing and civilizing the world. These merchant venturers of five thousand years ago were 'the Children of the Sun'.

But why, some people asked, did they set out on these extraordinary world travels? The answer given by Elliot Smith was in terms of the Givers of Life formula, and we had best give it here in his own words. 'In delving into the remotely distant history of our species,' he wrote in *The Evolution of the Dragon*, we cannot fail to be impressed with the persistence with which, throughout the whole of his career, man ... has been seeking ... for an elixir of life to give added 'vitality' to the dead ... to prolong the days of active life to the living, to restore growth and to protect his own life from all assaults, not merely of time but also of circumstance.

These world travellers were then, according to Elliot Smith and Perry, looking for elixirs, for what they called collectively 'givers of life'. They set out from Egypt and reached almost everywhere. There was no civilization before Egypt, at least no civilization that was not derived from Egypt. Elliot Smith immediately crossed swords with ethnologists in America because to him the Central American civilizations were certainly derived from Egypt. Everything started in Egypt – everything. When he was once asked what was taking place in the cultural development of the world when Egypt was allegedly laying the foundations of civilization, he answered at once 'Nothing'. Perry's comment on this statement is flabbergasting in its naïveté and ignorance. 'The accumulation of fresh evidence during the twenty-odd years that have since elapsed has tended to confirm the essential accuracy of what was then an astonishing generalization.' Those are Perry's very words; at least we can be in agreement with the phrase 'astonishing generalization'.

We do not want to spend too long in discussing the authors of this pan-Egyptian hyperdiffusion theory. Elliot Smith and Perry really abandoned any pretence at scientific method. They did not evaluate the evidence and arrive at a theory. Elliot Smith had been swept away by Egypt, he had been convinced by mummies and megaliths, his theory was formed and everything was squeezed into this theory – circumstances of time, place, and function were brushed aside with airy condescension. Lowie is not a whit too sharp, not an iota too cruel when he says of the astonishing development of the Elliot Smith theories:

Here there is no humble quest of the truth, no patient scrutiny of difficulties, no attempt to understand sincere criticism. Vehement reiteration takes the place of argument . . . Everything is grist for his mill, everything is either black or white . . . In physical anthropology Elliot Smith controls the facts hence, right or wrong – his judgements command respect while in ethnography his crass ignorance darkens counsel.*

Nor is Lowie too severe when he refers to 'the unfathomable ignorance of elementary ethnography' displayed by Elliot Smith and Perry.† In a lecture on *Conversion in Science* which Elliot Smith gave in 1928 at the Imperial College of Science – it was the Huxley Memorial Lecture – he said this: 'The set attitude of mind of a scholar may become almost indistinguishable from a delusion.' He was not, quite naturally, thinking of himself when he wrote this sentence, but this is unfortunately just what had happened to him. He had acquired a set attitude of mind with regard to the Egyptian origin of all culture, and it had become a delusion.

To us at the present day it is a distraction to look back at this pan-Egyptian diffusionist delusion but its significance is much more than an amusing sidelight on the development of ideas of prehistory. For the Elliot Smith–Perry school were not alone in their search for a simple all-embracing solution. Elliot Smith died in 1937. Two years later Lord Raglan published his *How Came Civilization*. Raglan is still with us and writing but he corresponds in his essential philosophical basis with Elliot Smith and Perry. He does not believe in the possibility of inventions being made twice. Let us quote his views.

No invention, discovery, custom, belief, or even story is known for certain to have originated in two separate cultures . . . The natural state of man is a state of low savagery . . . towards that state he always tends to revert whenever he is not checked, or forced in the opposite direction, by that unexplained, but highly artificial localized

* R. H. Lowie, *The History of Ethnological Theory*, pp. 60–61.
† ibid., p. 166.

PLATE I : FRERE'S HAND AXES

'. . . evidently weapons of war, fabricated and used by a people who had not the use of metals . . . the situation in which these weapons were found may tempt us to refer them to a very remote period indeed, even beyond that of the present world.' JOHN FRERE

Schliemann 'by digging in the ground made Homer come alive in the dusty hillside of the Troad and later at Mycenae. He had created a fresh chapter in the human past, had himself written prehistory.'

'From the end of Victorian days Upper Palaeolithic art was part of the perspective of prehistory.'

Dr Williams Freeman 'once said to Crawford that "one ought to be a bird to
be a field archaeologist". The development of aircraft and of aerial photography
during and after the 1914–18 war enabled archaeologists virtually to become
birds.'

a IN CORNWALL

b IN PORTUGAL

'. . . the megalithic tombs of western Europe. In the nineteenth century the likenesses between megalithic tombs from Denmark and the Orkneys to Iberia and the Mediterranean were appreciated. . . .'

PLATE 6 : TOLLUND MAN

'Very rarely we are given special clues: the bodies in the Danish peat-bogs like Tollund preserve for us the oldest examples of flesh in prehistory.'

'... there are representations of human beings in early art but they give us little in the way of racial characteristics to go on.'

'... the pleasure of prehistory is in the recovery of the treasures of man's prehistoric past that have been dropped on the way and lost ... we can today admire and enjoy the brilliant simplicity and purity of line of the stylized Cycladic figurines.'

and spasmodic process which we know as the progress of civilization ... savages never invent or discover anything ... many of the principal discoveries and inventions upon which our civilization is based can be traced with considerable probability to an area with its focus near the head of the Persian Gulf, and such evidence as there is suggests that they were made by ingenious priests as a means of facilitating the performance of religious ritual.*

Lord Raglan allows a great civilizing process to take place in the sixteenth century A.D. but this is only the second time in man's whole history, and his general conclusion remains that 'civilization then, far from being a process that keeps going on everywhere, is really an event which has only happened twice'.† Raglan has done little more than substitute Sumeria for Egypt, and this is also what Heine-Geldern has done, and nervously realizes he has done, in the number of *Diogenes* devoted to the work of Toynbee.

Now why does the world tolerate this academic rubbish from people like Elliot Smith, Perry, and Raglan? There are many reasons. First there is a deep-seated desire for a simple answer to complicated problems.‡ That is why the earlier pre-archaeological prehistorians clutched at the Trojans, the Phoenicians, the Lost Tribes of Israel, the Druids, and, let us particularly not forget in this present context, the Egyptians. The Ancient Egyptians as the saviours of the world were invented long before Elliot Smith was made Professor of Anatomy in Cairo. And this simplistic easy solution to prehistory is still something which people hanker after. I have little doubt that the cult of Atlantis at the present day is a part of this, and the sale of books explaining how all civilization came from the vanished island of Atlantis, or Mu, or Lake Titicaca, or Heligoland is a proof of it. These theories are still widely canvassed at the present day and the books dealing with them sell well,

* Lord Raglan, *How Came Civilization?* 1939, pp. 15, 38.

† ibid., p. 182.

‡ On this see R. Crawshay Williams, *The Comforts of Unreason*, 1947, *passim*.

and one is always being asked about Atlantis and Titicaca just as one is asked about Phoenicians and the Lost Tribes of Israel.

It is often said by professional archaeological scholars that we should not concern ourselves unduly with what is after all only one aspect of the rather large lunatic fringe of prehistory, that we have far better things to do advancing the true path of knowledge and accumulating by archaeological means the basic facts to be distilled out of prehistory, and that most of these extraordinary books giving single origins to man's civilization in one great movement or event or spread of culture-heroes are beneath contempt. There is much in this, but here we *are* concerned with the ideas people have or want to have about prehistory, and there is no doubt that many have had and want to have the simple solutions of an Elliot Smith, a Raglan, a Bellamy, or a Spanuth. This is not merely because, as I have said, there seems a deep-seated desire for a simple all-embracing explanation but because the gradual elaboration and complication of the archaeological record has begun to bewilder people. It was all right in Victorian times when you could read Lubbock's *Prehistoric Times* or in Edwardian times when you read Rice Holmes's *Ancient Britain and the Invasions of Julius Caesar*, all right when the prehistoric past of man seemed an easily assimilable tale of Palaeolithic, Neolithic, Bronze Age, and Early Iron Age, but not all right when you began to read the complicated story which prehistorians offer at the present day with its extraordinarily complicated sequences of cultures in different areas. Look for example at any chart at the end of Childe's *Dawn of European Civilization* or of Christopher Hawkes's *Prehistoric Foundations of Europe*, at the chart at the end of Stuart Piggott's *Neolithic Cultures of the British Isles*, and you may well be pardoned if you recoil from the complicated archaeological constructs which seem to have replaced the simple succession which the Victorians so gladly elaborated into the not so complicated succession advocated by de Mortillet and which was set out by MacCurdy in his *Human Origins* and Burkitt in his *Prehistory*.

It is then we suggest, as part of a desire for a simple all-embracing solution, and as part of a reaction from the complexity of the archaeological record, that we should look at the distractions of this hyperdiffusionism which beset the fringes of our discipline from Miss Buckland to Mr Bellamy.

It needs emphasizing here that the error lies in the simplistic hyperdiffusion of the one-centre school, just as the Victorian unilinear system of cultural evolution was an error. Neither diffusion nor evolution itself as an explanation of cultural change is an error; the error has lain in the extravagant interpretation of cultural change in terms of only one of these explanations and that taken to obsessional extremes. In the new prehistory which was coming into being in the twenties diffusion was the accepted explanation of cultural change in archaeology. The man who was perhaps most responsible for slowly and surely putting across a modified diffusionism was Gordon Childe in his *Dawn of European Civilization* (1925), his *Danube in Prehistory* (1929), and his *Bronze Age* (1930). In these books we see developing the climate of the new prehistory which carefully builds up the details of the succession of cultures in each area and sees cultures or elements of cultures spreading from one area to another. This diffusionism is not open to the charges levelled – and very correctly – at the hyperdiffusionist school, namely that it neglected all semblance of scientific methods.

In our own modern prehistory the Childe and Childe-derivative archaeologists are working in the best traditions of scientific method. Before two cultural objects or traditions are compared it is made certain that they are functionally and formally identical. It is one of the great confusions of the Elliot Smith–Perry school of hyperdiffusion that they never made sure that the objects they were comparing were functionally and formally identical; they rashly compared the

Pyramids of Egypt with the Pyramids of Central America, monuments which are admittedly superficially identical, without realizing that while the Egyptian pyramids were tombs, the American pyramids were great temple platforms on the top of which religious rites were performed. The diffusionists of the new prehistory do not make these mistakes; they compare only cultural features which are formally and functionally identical and only derive the one from the other if such a historical process can be shown to be chronologically, geographically, and historically possible.

Let me take as an example of the modified Childe diffusionism of the twenties, which had become standard archaeological theory in the thirties and forties, the megalithic tombs of western Europe. In the nineteenth century the likenesses between megalithic tombs from Denmark and the Orkneys to Iberia and the Mediterranean were appreciated, but there then seemed only one of two possible explanations for these likenesses (Plate 5). The first was that these monuments had come into existence naturally in different areas as part of the natural cultural evolution of man. The second view was that there was a great megalithic master race which spread from one centre – Denmark itself was sometimes canvassed, and at other times it was some unspecified area in the east Mediterranean – indeed at the present day the general view is to talk in fairly vague terms of an Aegean or Minoan–Mycenaean cultural spread. We have already seen how Elliot Smith and Perry took over this idea of a megalithic race which became part of their pan-Egyptian colonial movement.

But when one gets down to detailed analysis of the spread of megalithic tombs in the western Mediterranean and western Europe, one sees that no one facile explanation will suffice. In the first place megaliths do not represent a single unitary movement but contacts along the same routes over many centuries. Many scholars at the present day would date the first passage graves of Ireland and Brittany to the middle of the

third millennium B.C.* but it is equally clear to many who look
at the decorated entrance slab at New Grange that it must be
compared with the spirals and lozenges on the blocking slabs
at Castelluccio in Sicily, the Hal Tarxien slabs in Malta, and the
designs on the shaft-graves at Mycenae – all evidence of contact across Europe in the sixteenth or fifteenth century B.C.
Secondly, even if one allows initial movements of people with
a basic tomb type and a basic custom of collective burial, that
basic tomb type is probably a rock-cut tomb; megalithic
architecture may have arisen independently in the west Mediterranean in several places, Malta for instance and southern
Spain and southern France. Tomb types in these separate areas
developed often along parallel lines.

There has been in recent years an even greater revolution in
the generally accepted modified Childe diffusionism. Northern
antiquaries have for a long time classified the megalithic
tombs of Denmark, Sweden, and Germany into three successive groups, first the *dös* or *dysse* usually confusingly translated
into English as 'dolmen' – a word used in English in a very
wide variety of ways; secondly the passage grave, and thirdly
the long stone cist. Now while at first it was argued that these
three stages represented a simple evolutionary sequence in
northern Europe, the later diffusionist view was that each
stage represented a movement from some part of western
Europe and the west Mediterranean. The last stage characterized by the long stone cists was thought, for instance, to have
spread from the Paris basin somewhere between 1600 and
1400 B.C. and this is still a possibility; the second stage characterized by passage graves was, and indeed still is, seen as part of
the spread of passage graves in western Europe between 2500
and 1500 B.C. The first stage, that characterized by *dösar*, *dysser*,
or *dolmens*, was less easily explained but there were vague
parallels to these monuments in western Europe – various

* A date of 3000 B.C. has been suggested on Carbon-14 analysis for a passage
grave in Brittany by P. R. Giot (see *Antiquity*, 1959, p. 238).

archaeologists pointed hopefully, if a little uncertainly, at the polygonal dolmens of Portugal and the rectangular dolmens of the Pyrenean area. But now as the result of detailed researches by Professor Becker of Copenhagen we see the tombs of this first stage as something quite different, as the translation into megalithic architecture of earth graves that existed in northern Europe before; what is more, Professor Becker reminds us that these first-stage megalithic tombs are not collective tombs at all and never contained more than a few burials. It now looks as though we must accept the independent origin of some megalithic architecture in Denmark.

Very gradually we are entering on a new mid-twentieth-century stage in our ideas of the interpretation of prehistoric change: indeed after the distractions of the hyperdiffusionists and the fairly generally accepted reasonable doctrine of the modified diffusionists we are back to one of the Victorian positions when, said Lowie, as I have already quoted, 'evolution . . . lay down amicably beside Diffusion'.

There is now, then, a very considerable change going on in the view which people are beginning to have and express about the nature of cultural spread and change in prehistory. Yet some would say that while we may be forced to modify our views in detail on some points the overall picture is the same. The overall picture would appear to be something like this: that the elements of a higher food-producing civilization came into existence in the Near East in and around what Breasted called the Fertile Crescent, and that the elements of this culture complex spread all over the world, not of course diffused by a master race, but by varying peoples in varying stages. Perhaps there were two great stages, the earliest of which was called by Childe the Neolithic Revolution of, perhaps, ten thousand years ago, and the second the Urban Revolution of five thousand years ago which produced urban literate communities in Egypt and Mesopotamia. This was the picture painted in Gordon Childe's *What Happened in History* and *Man Makes Himself*, and in the series of books written by H. J. E. Peake and H. J. Fleure called *The Corridors of Time*. The first volume of *The Corridors of Time* was published under the title *Apes and Men* in 1927, and the tenth and last volume, called *Times and Places*, in 1956; Peake had himself died in 1946. Now Peake and Fleure were not Elliot Smith–Perry diffusionists, indeed Peake used to say with a twinkle that he found it difficult to look at the world through a Perryscope. But the Peake and Fleure books on which my generation of archaeologists was brought up, admirably demonstrate the modified Childe diffusionism of the twenties and thirties.

Let me quote from the preface to the last volume, *Times and Places*.

It has been the writers' belief in compiling the *Corridors* that south-west Asia was the region in which man made the great step forward from dependence on hunting and collecting to food-production by cereal cultivation; and to this the keeping of domestic animals was soon added. While there may have been small attempts at cultivation begun independently elsewhere, and there were probably several more or less independent beginnings of the domestication of animals, the spread of food-production from south-west Asia and Egypt and its consequences remain major features of the story of mankind.

Now this is very true, but how major is another story which Peake and Fleure omit entirely from their ten-volume essay down the corridors of time, and this omission is deliberate and planned. 'The Americas,' they write, 'with their largely distinct problems have not been included in the survey.' But the problem of prehistory is the problem of the prehistory of man, not the prehistory of the Old World. We find the same refusal to study the American evidence in Gordon Childe's *What Happened in History*. Yet the story of New World cultural origins is of paramount importance to our study of Old World cultural origins.

The Western World learned about the Americas for the first

time in 1492 when Christopher Columbus discovered America
when looking for the Indies. The subsequent explorers of
Central America 'succeeded in doing', to quote Carleton
Coon's words, 'something every archaeologist dreams of
which is to step backwards in time . . . they marched into an
Early Metal Age civilization comparable in many respects
with that of Egypt in late Predynastic or early Dynastic times,
and that of earliest Sumeria'.★ Since then historians and
archaeologists have wanted to find out how this civilization
came into existence and what relation it bore to the civilizations
of the ancient world. The Spanish found themselves in the New
World face to face with the Aztecs of Mexico who met them
in battle with composite weapons of obsidian blades set in
grooved wood, and the Mayas of Yucatan, Guatemala, and the
Honduras who built elaborate temples and pyramids and who
had no metal at all except a few gold and copper ornaments,
and the Incas of Peru who had complicated networks of roads
like the Roman roads, suspension bridges of rope, and domesticated animals – the llama, the alpaca, and the guinea-pig. All
these three native American civilizations – Aztecs, Mayas, and
Incas – were based on agriculture. And both the Aztecs and
Mayas as well as other American Indians in Mexico could
write; they had a pictographic script which they wrote in
deerskin books.

How had all this come about? Of course Christopher Columbus was not the first European to visit America. Leif Ericsson
got to Greenland and Vinland in A.D. 1001. It is not suggested
that Leif Ericsson introduced the elements of higher civilization to America, but it has been the fashion to suggest that
someone did do this, and, of course, particularly the fashion
by those who could not bring themselves to believe that anything could be invented or discovered on more than one
occasion. While there has been a fashion, there has been no
agreement on who brought (or was thought to have brought)

★ Carleton S. Coon, *The History of Man*, 1955, p. 344.

the higher civilization to America. To some they were Phoenicians or the Lost Tribes of Israel, to others Welshmen like Madoc or Irishmen like St Brandon, to other Negroes from Africa, Japanese, Polynesians, or people from the supposed and supposedly sunken continents of Atlantis, Lemuria, or Mu – or of course if you were looking at prehistory through a Perryscope, it was brought by the ancient Egyptians themselves. It is really the old problem that we discussed in our first lecture; we are back in the legendary epoch of prehistoric research.

That may be so, but in studying American cultural origins we are engaged in what is almost a controlled laboratory experiment. That is why American prehistory is so important to the prehistorian working in Europe or the Near East or India. We are now in a position to give objective answers to American prehistoric chronology – answers based first on dendrochronological researches but latterly on Carbon-14 analysis. The Carbon-14 dates in the Bat Cave in New Mexico show that American Indians were growing maize by 4000 B.C. Further comparative analysis and study shows that almost every cultural element in the New World can be explained as of purely local growth. There are still some puzzles – the gourd, cotton, the sweet potato, and Indian corn are among them – but on the whole the story as it looks at this moment is that about 10,000 B.C. man came to America probably across a dry Bering Straits, and that by 5000 B.C. all of the New World except the Eskimo country was occupied. By 4000 B.C. agriculture had begun in the New World and in due course these early agricultural communities developed into the Urban Civilizations of Central America; and at the moment it looks as though this development happened in America without any contact of a serious nature from abroad. It was in fact a tale of independent cultural evolution.

If this was so in America, we now ask, why not elsewhere in the Old World? Rice cultivation probably developed

independently in south China when wheat and barley were being cultivated in the Near East and maize in America. Indeed it is
probably true that we have been creating our own difficulties
to a certain extent, and inventing the problems of diffusion
versus local evolution by conceptualizing certain ideas. Agriculture and civilization are two such ideas; we talk about the
origins of 'agriculture' and discuss whether 'it' started in the
Near East and spread from there to China, India, and America
when all the time what we should be talking about is the discovery of the cultivation of wheat and barley in Egypt, Palestine, and Iraq, of rice in eastern India and south China, and of
maize and squash in Central America. We have created our
own problems by grouping together all these material advances in culture under one word 'agriculture'. And it is to a
certain extent the same with 'civilization'. We describe
civilizations in Egypt, Sumeria, the Indus Valley, China, and
Central America and ask how they came into existence,
flourished, and decayed, and what was their genetic inter-
relationship – without perhaps realizing that because all these
societies had writing and cities and a high skill in metal-working they are not necessarily connected.

It would seem, then, that we have travelled a long way from
the earlier diffusionists to our present very modified diffusionism with its recognition of the real existence of independent
evolution; perhaps that long way had to involve the distractions of the hyperdiffusionists. I said in the previous lectures,
that the development of the prehistoric record had brought us
to a stage where we were studying the development of cultures
in time and space, that we were studying a gaily coloured
layer cake. The first concern of prehistoric archaeology was the
study of the chronological and spatial position of these layers.
It was also, secondarily, the study of their interrelations if the
time–space positions permitted such interrelationships; this
study, which after all is the only way in which we can begin to
understand cultural change and its complex mechanics, is one

we should undertake without any preconceived ideas of diffusion and independent invention.

We should approach this study of cultural origins and change at the present day with the lessons of American prehistory very much in mind, for here it does seem that man developed from the Mesolithic food-gathering savages of the end of the Ice Age through to the literate urban communities of Central America without significant contacts observable in the archaeological record from the Old World of Europe and Africa on the one hand or Asia and Indonesia on the other. If there is one lesson more than any other which mid-twentieth-century research is forcibly injecting into our idea of prehistory it is that of the independent development of prehistoric American culture. The news of the early dating by Carbon-14 of the first American agricultural communities has come like a tremendous blast of cold wind blowing down the corridors of time where walked scholars who seemed to have arrived at a fixed picture of world prehistory and cultural origins in terms of Neolithic and Urban Revolutions in the Near East.

CHAPTER SIX

THE IDEA OF PREHISTORY IN THE STUDY OF LANGUAGE AND RACE, AND IN POLITICS

WE have seen how prehistoric archaeology came into existence as a new perspective of the human past – as an extension backward of ancient history and forward of geology, and how by the second quarter of the twentieth century prehistory had developed its own expertise, both in methods and results. The main result seemed to be a gaily coloured layer or Neapolitan cake which changed as one turned the cake round. This was the complicated space–time cataloguing of cultures. We have also seen that the first task of the prehistorian seemed to be the listing and definition of these cultures and his second the study of the nature of their interrelations. I hope we have seen, too, that, as the twentieth century advanced, no simple explanation in terms of independent cultural evolution or of diffusion unilaterally from one centre was really acceptable, but what was and is acceptable is the notion that the development of cultures in prehistory (as in historic times) is a complicated process in which independent evolutionary forces and outside influences both play important parts.

It was not surprising that, as prehistoric archaeology developed, scholars should begin to say that it seemed to be becoming an arid discipline of cultural listing, or a sort of archaeological cultural chess. The question was asked, was the prehistoric archaeologist going to tell us no more about the prehistoric past than the lateral and vertical moves on a three-dimensional chess-board? Was all we were going to get out of research in prehistory a catalogue of changes in material culture? These questions were asked particularly sharply by archaeologists interested in the findings of neighbouring disciplines like geography, anthropology, and history, and from the human geographers, anthropologists, and historians themselves interested in this aspect of the human past. There were also the language scholars, the linguistic palaeontologists, and others who were themselves concerned in certain aspects of very early human history.

Let us take first the linguists and the physical anthropologists; they were concerned with the facts of language and race and were asking how their conjectural history of language and race fitted in to the record of prehistory, and also what new and definitive answers could prehistory give about the origins of language and race.

Now language is a cultural feature of man, but it only becomes apprehended by the archaeologist who is studying the material culture of man when it becomes material, i.e. when it is written down on coins, stones, or books. We are here concerned with prehistoric times – the times when there was no writing on coins, stone, and books: we deal with preliterate times, so that one might say that, *ipso facto*, the prehistorian cannot tell anything about the spread and diffusion of languages. The prehistorian cannot answer you when you say, 'When was the Celtic language introduced into Great Britain?' Or, more specifically, 'Is it true that the Q-Celtic languages now surviving in Irish, Scots Gaelic, and Manx were introduced into the British Isles before (or long before) the P-Celtic languages which survive in Welsh and Breton, and survived until recently in Cornish?'

It is unfortunately not quite so simple as that. If as prehistorians we could wash our hands of linguistic equations and problems we would be happier: if we could just say, well, no language survives from any prehistoric culture so we can tell you nothing, all would be well. As it is we cannot do this. The great family of languages variously referred to as the Aryan, Indo–European, or Indo–Germanic languages came into existence somewhere between Eastern Europe and the Himalaya, somewhere north of the Turkish–Armenian–Iranian mountain barrier, perhaps on the plains of Hungary, the Ukraine, or Turkestan. The speakers of this basic Indo–European language and its derivative languages like Sanskrit, Celtic, Slav, Greek, Latin, and the rest of them spread out from this area all over Europe and south-west Asia and into India where Aryan-speaking peoples (here the noble caste actually called themselves Aryas) overran and destroyed the urban Bronze Age literate civilization of Harappa and Mohenjo–Daro. It is often argued that the material culture of these Aryan speakers ought to be identifiable and that we should be able to say of a collection of tools and weapons, here are the material remains of the Aryans.

There is a great difficulty here. An invasion of people as seen in a sudden change in the material culture of a region does not necessarily betoken a change in the language spoken. The reverse is often true: a new language may be introduced into a country and there is no apparent evidence for the appearance of new people as shown by new material cultural traits in the archaeological record. The Norman Conquest of England and Wales on the one hand and the conquest of Brittany in the fifth to seventh centuries A.D. by settlers from South-west England and Wales are good proofs of these statements. We do not speak Norman-French in England although there is plenty of archaeological evidence of the material culture of the Normans in England; the Breton language is a version of Old Welsh or Old British but there is hardly a trace in the material culture of fifth- to seventh-century Brittany of the arrival of these new speakers from Britain. It is very difficult to argue correlations for invading cultures in linguistic terms and the archaeologists who say that the Beaker Folk spoke Q-Celtic or the Late Bronze Age invaders of Britain spoke

P-Celtic are extending possibilities into facts and treating very tentative hypotheses as proven.

But do not think that what I am saying is a counsel of despair. Let us look at the Iberian peninsula. Here at the time of the Roman conquest were tribes, mainly in the north and north-west, who spoke Celtic languages; these people must have come into Iberia from outside France, and if there is to be an archaeological component to these people it cannot be any people before the urn-field invaders of the late Bronze Age and early Iron Age – people who came into Spain between 850 and 600 B.C. and the distribution of whose material remains agrees quite well with that of the Celtic place-names and Celtic tribes of Spain. Here in Iberia is a legitimate and valuable correlation that can be made between the archaeological invasions of the prehistorian and the facts of the student of languages. We can in Spain go a little further. Here there exists a language – Basque – unlike any other in Europe; it must have been there before the arrival of the Indo-European speakers who introduced Celtic into Iberia. If this was so, and it is difficult to argue any other case, then Basque must be the survival of a Bronze Age language spoken in Spain and south France. We cannot go any further than this but it is not impossible that Basque was the language of some of the Neolithic–Chalcolithic tomb builders of south-west France and north Spain in the early second millennium B.C.

We cannot really go so far as this, and indeed seldom can we go so far as we have done in Spain. We cannot for example say who introduced the Q-Celtic language into Ireland or who really introduced the Greek language into Greece or the Italic tongues into Italy. This is quite naturally one of the frustrations of prehistory – one of the very many frustrations – or should one say that it is one of the defining limitations of prehistory?

The same sort of problem is found when we come to deal with the problems of race. Race to the anthropologist is a group of people with physical characteristics in common – inherited physical characteristics that is – and though we may not agree with this or that classification of race, we do not, without any training in the mysteries of physical anthropology, have any difficulty in distinguishing the Nordic type with its tall stature, blue eyes, fair hair, and fair skin, from the Bushman with his kinky hair, black skin, short stature, and steatopygia. Any ordinary political cartoonist quite untrained in measuring heads and working out cephalic indexes has no difficulty in drawing a Negro and a Chinaman as different racial portraits. The various races of man developed in the last few thousand years, and it is reasonable to suppose that in the past, that is to say in the remote prehistoric past, when human groups were not in such close contact with each other as in later phases of history and were mating from the same sort of stocks, geographical groups of people were more racially pure than they are at the present day. If this is so then, it has been argued, cannot the cultures of the prehistorians be given some more semblance of reality by a description of the physical appearance of the people? Can we not in the earlier phases of prehistory equate physical types with cultural groups? Can we not say that the so-called warrior cultures of northern Europe – the people who buried their dead in single graves with battle axes in the second quarter of the second millennium B.C. – were created by people who belonged to the Nordic type?

There is inherently here a methodological difficulty, and an obvious one like that involved in the tracing backwards of language groups. It is that the fleshy parts of our prehistoric ancestors do not survive; the hair, eyes, and skin on which so much of racial classification is based and by which we ourselves so easily describe racial types, do not survive. Very rarely are we given special clues: the bodies in the Danish peatbogs like Tollund preserve for us the oldest examples of flesh in prehistory (Plate 6), and the older bodies from the

Danish tree-coffins of the Bronze Age are also of some value in determining racial types.

There are also representations of human beings in early art (Plate 7) but they give us little in the way of racial characteristics to go on until we come to the Egyptians who in the nineteenth dynasty decorated the walls of the royal tombs with representations of the four races of mankind, namely the Egyptians themselves whom they painted red, the Asiatics whom they painted yellow, the Southerners or Negroes whom they naturally represented black, and a fourth type, the Libyans, Westerners, or Northerners whom they represented as white with blue eyes and fair beards. Even this information, imprecise though it is, goes back only three thousand years.

A second factor which vitally affects any attempt we make to take man's racial history back and to equate aspects of it with archaeologically derived facts is that it is not only the fleshy parts that do not survive; sometimes nothing survives at all. Whole skeletons – bone as well as the mantle of flesh – may disappear in acid soils, and the moment cremation became a general custom, as it was, for example, extensively in the Middle and Late Bronze Ages in Britain, we were left with nothing at all to assist our study of the physical remains of man except a heap of ashes. It is, then, not really possible to say a great deal about the physical types of early man, but we can make a few useful generalizations. The type of person normally found in megalithic tombs in north-western Europe, for example, has a skeleton not far removed from that standard in the so-called Mediterranean race. This is not a surprising fact in reality, when we consider that most of the builders of these tombs spread up into northern and north-western Europe from the Mediterranean. This may be as far as we can go; and yet, perhaps, not quite – the population of Ireland, for example, is probably most extensively derived from that of the megalithic builders and it is tempting on this ground and on the identity of the megalithic builders skeletally with the present-day Mediterranean race to see their bones clothed with a sallow skin, their eye-sockets filled with dark eyes, and the tops of their long heads covered with black hair.

The existence of this Mediterranean type in our Neolithic and Chalcolithic communities of megalithic and non-megalithic types in the British Isles is quite beyond dispute and it contrasts very markedly with the Beaker type found in inhumed single graves of the Early Bronze Age in Britain – tall, strongly built types with robust, squarish faces.

Thus far we can go in correlating the facts of archaeology and physical anthropology; no further than in the correlation of facts of archaeology and linguistic history. And, as we think about it, we see that it is not really very far. Race, language, and culture are, as we well know in the modern world, separate ways of classifying and grouping men. The Jews, for example, were until recently a detribalized nation bound together at least in part by religious ties; they were a cultural unit not necessarily speaking the same language though they preserved Hebrew in a modified form in Judeo-German or Yiddish, and not necessarily belonging to the same race although people in western Europe, whose only acquaintance with the racial types of the Middle East was through seeing Jews, thought they did form a racial group. When we see, as in this example of the Jews, how very clearly it is impossible to equate racial, linguistic, and cultural groupings in modern times when we have very full documentation to assist us, we see it is a hopeless task to try to do it in prehistoric times when we have no written sources, when we have to judge language facts by later distributions of place-names and our physical types are often skeletons or jars of ashes from funeral pyres.

The idea of prehistory which we must now have with regard to the early spread of races and languages must essentially, except in a few rare cases, be separated from our ideas of cultures. We must alas, for the most part, keep the builders and bearers of our prehistoric cultures speechless and physically neutral. This may seem to you an unsatisfying conclusion. And so it is but then much of our prehistory is unsatisfying and difficult, tantalizingly meagre and sketchy. We can appreciate this and accept the limitations of prehistory along with its excitements. But what is good enough for you and me – this hard scholarly doctrine – was not good enough for the politicians and propagandists who, in the last quarter-century, have been using the facts or apparent facts of prehistory to confuse the public.

They have done this because the facts could so easily be grafted on to the apparent facts of racism. Now racism of course is something very different from race. To quote the late Ruth Benedict's neat statement on racism:

Racism is not, like race, a subject the content of which can be scientifically investigated. It is like a religion, a belief that can be studied only historically. Like any belief that goes beyond scientific knowledge it can be judged only by its fruits and by its votaries and its ulterior purposes.*

Racism is the dogma that one race or one ethnic group for that matter is superior, other races or groups inferior, and that indeed the superiority and inferiority is something congenital, something to which people are condemned or blessed by nature. It is of course a comforting and comfortable doctrine for those said to be the superiors. It is, also of course, entirely wrong; it is a form of racial modern superstition. Most of us remember vividly how racism was made a principal basis of German polity. But all this started long before Nazi politics.

The classic statement of racism is by the Comte de Gobineau who between 1853 and 1857 wrote his *Essay on the Inequality of Human Races*. Gobineau was a Frenchman and he was really developing the ideas of Boulainvilliers – the Comte de Boulainvilliers – who argued that the nobles of France, the

* Ruth Benedict, *Race and Racism*, 1942, p. 131.

survivors of the feudal aristocracy, were the remains of the Germani, the Teutonic barbarians who had overrun the Roman Empire, while the populace of France was of quite a different racial clay. The populace were the old Gallo-Roman stock of France; racially Mediterranean and linguistically Celts. They were, according to Boulainvilliers, destined to racial inferiority as the Franks were to racial superiority. The Comte de Gobineau – and I always feel that it is not insignificant that these doctrines were being developed by two members of what was supposed to be the racially superior element in France – developed Boulainvilliers's ideas. He taught that the hope of the world, not merely the hope of France, lay, and indeed always had lain, with the fair-haired Teutons; and he was now calling these people *Aryans*. It was the current fashion to call them this, and what he meant, of course, though imprecisely, was what physical anthropologists would, at the present day, call the Nordic race.

Perhaps I should re-emphasize here that there is nothing imprecise and nothing wrong in the idea of the Aryans; it is a precise linguistic term, in origin and in present usage linguistic. It is the extension of this linguistic term to include racial characteristics – those of the Nordic race – that was the first confusion; and the second that these Aryan-Nordics were superior, were the leaders of the world. It was not meant to be a succession of confusions in the Comte de Gobineau's writings; far from it. He was not engaged in deliberate confusions; he was merely unable to think straight about these matters. But it was meant to be a confusion by the time it became an accepted part of Nazi policy because its progenitors and advocates did not want to think straight, nor want their deluded followers to think straight; and after all nobody who bothered to analyse the Nazi-superiority–Aryan-Nordic myth and then to think of the fair-haired Teutons could come to any flattering conclusions about the racial affinities of many of the German political leaders from Hitler downwards.

The really interesting thing about the Comte de Gobineau is that he was not preaching a nationalist doctrine of racialist prehistory. His theme was international, was pan-European in scope. He dedicated his *Essay on the Inequality of Human Races* to George V of Hanover, and this is what he wrote himself about the whole problem:

Gradually I have become convinced that race overshadows all other problems in history, that it holds the key to them all, and that the inequality of people from whose fusion a people is formed is enough to explain the whole course of its destiny. I convinced myself at last that everything great, noble, and fruitful in the works of man on this earth in science, art, and civilization derives from a single starting point; it belongs to one family alone, the different branches of which have reigned in all the civilized countries of the universe.

Gobineau was, as indeed all out-and-out racialists preaching about a master race must be, a hyperdiffusionist – in many ways like the hyperdiffusionists we spoke about in the last lecture such as Miss Buckland, Sir Grafton Elliot Smith, W. J. Perry, and Lord Raglan. But the cultural hyperdiffusionists demanded a master people; Gobineau's was a master *race*. He had divided the world into the whites, yellows, and blacks; his 'fair-haired Teuton-Aryans' were the only representatives of the white race and he was therefore forced to classify the Alpines of Central and Eastern Europe as yellow, or of yellow extraction, and the Mediterraneans as of black extraction! Of course Gobineau was writing in the early 1850s before the publication of *The Origin of Species*, and well before the development of scientific physical anthropology with its accurate measurements and classifications.

Gobineau was a Frenchman but the Germans were not slow to adopt his racial views, or a modification of them. Richard Wagner found Gobineau's work excellent and popularized his writings in Germany. The *Gobineau Vereinigung* was founded in 1894: and five years later Wagner's son-in-law Houston Stewart Chamberlain published his *The Foundations of the Nineteenth Century*. It was actually published in German at Munich that year; the English translation appeared in 1911. These two large volumes made Gobinism a cult and an important cult in Germany. The Kaiser read them aloud to his sons, had them distributed to officers of the army, and directed that they should be displayed in bookshops and in public libraries throughout Germany. Chamberlain's book went through edition after edition and without any doubt whatsoever became part of the underlying unconscious assumptions of the German nation – or of a large part of it.

Houston Chamberlain had to operate and propagate his racialist doctrines at a time when a great deal was becoming known about physical anthropology, and he could not go on insisting that the master race was one of tall, blond, fair-skinned, blue-eyed giants. So they were just called Teutons, but they were not Teutons in the strict sense of people who spoke a Teutonic language: there were Celts and Slavs also in this 'single pure stock' which were the original great ones, the really chosen people: but some were brunette and broad-headed and others blond dolichocephalics. But as his doctrines were accepted and developed there was a steady shift away from even a prejudiced and confused physical anthropology; in the end it was all a *mystique* – a *mystique* of the Great German Race versus the rest and particularly against the Jews, that, following Houston Chamberlain, were confusingly called Semites. Now it is true that Hebrew is a Semitic language, but there are many other Semitic languages, notably Arabic. The use of the phrase Semitic in a pejorative sense was part of the denigration of the Jews as anti-Master-race people. We can see how far Houston Chamberlain had himself gone towards this racialist *mystique* when, for example, he says: 'Whoever reveals himself German by his acts, whatever his genealogical tree, is a German,' and again, 'One can very soon become a Jew ... it needs only to have frequent intercourse with Jews or to read Jewish newspapers.'

Small wonder, when one reads ridiculous sentences like this, that though *The Foundations of the Nineteenth Century* was received with such signal honour in Germany it remains 'among the most confused, pretentious and over-written books that racism has produced'.* Small wonder, too, that the Nazis took over these ideals which the Kaiser had read aloud to his sons. *Mein Kampf* absorbed it, and liked getting round the obvious difficulties of physical appearance in German leaders by the Chamberlain trick of 'a German soul in a non-German body'. How far we have got from physical appearance if we begin talking about souls.

Even so there were difficulties; the German opposition to Communism meant that the Slavs had to be dropped out of the master race stock of the chosen people; and after the Rome–Berlin axis was invented, it too had to be given a racialist basis and the Mediterranean race had to be looked at a little more charitably, although a great deal of emphasis could be and was laid on the Germanness of northern Italy.

Because I have deliberately taken the main development of racialist theory from Gobineau to Chamberlain and Alfred Rosenberg, this must not be taken to mean that it was only the Germans who had this exaggerated racialist master race myth at the basis of their thought. It existed also in America, and the best and classic example of American racialists was Madison Grant – the man who in 1917 produced his remarkable book *The Passing of the Great Race*. The thesis of this book is a very simple one, and there is hardly any need to mention at this stage who the great race was – it was our old friend the Nordic Teuton leaders, and Madison Grant said very outspokenly: 'The amount of Nordic blood in each nation is a very fair measure of its strength in war and its standing in civilization.' So far, so good, the Gobineau French and German racialists might say, but as they read on through *The*

* These words are those of Ruth Benedict in her *Race and Racism*, London, 1942, p. 131.

Passing of the Great Race they had to exclaim 'but no further', because Grant's thesis was that the Germans and French of today were the descendants of the peasants, and that the Great Race of Nordic Teuton leaders had left Europe and were now in America. Even in 1917 Madison Grant was prepared to insist uncritically that the majority of Americans were Nordic; he declared that that moment was the chance for America to capture the glorious position of leadership which Europe had lost. Henry Fairfield Osborn, the doyen of American archaeology and anthropology at that time, wrote a preface to Grant's book in which he said that what America should do was to prevent 'the gradual dying out among our people of those hereditary traits through which the principles of our religious, political, or social foundations were laid down and to stop their insidious replacement by traits of less noble character'. Other American racialist books were even more inept, preaching the patriotic duty of Nordic racial hygiene.

We had something of this kind, but the other way round, in England, where it became a denigration not a praising of the Nordic-Teutons. There were ancient historians who saw the Germans in 1914 'what they were fifteen centuries ago – the barbarians who raided our ancestors and destroyed the civilization of the Roman Empire'. But no one was a patch in this matter on the German racialists, who harnessed prehistory to their racial-mad chariot and did so because they felt somehow that history must be or must be made to be on their side. 'The one and only thing that matters to us,' Heinrich Himmler is supposed to have said, 'and the thing these people are paid for by the state, is to have ideas of history that strengthen our people in their national pride.' And here of course prehistory, where we really know so little and guess so much, came into its Germanic own.

In 1939 courses in prehistoric archaeology were given in no less than twenty-five German universities, and archaeological research was lavishly supported by the Nazi State. Professor

Hermann Schneider of the University of Tübingen writing in 1939 said this:

The year 1933 witnessed the victory of an attitude towards the history of the culture of Germany which gave to the Germanic element of all that is German a significance previously unthought of. The best of what is German is Germanic and must be found in pure form in early Germanic times. Archaeological research thus found itself faced with the pleasant task of examining and reconstructing the real essence of Germanic life and customs.

These were the words of a Professor at Tübingen; if a Professor alleged this much, how much more were politicians ready to employ racialism and derive support for their doctrines from the prehistoric record. Himmler said: 'Prehistory is the doctrine of the eminence of the Germans at the dawn of civilization.' Here we have naked and unashamed the political view of prehistory.

It might well be thought that such a doctrine could hardly be sustained for long even in Nazi political circles, merely by constant reiteration. But there were unfortunately not lacking prehistorians who would supply necessary information for supporting these doctrines. The best – or worst – exponent of this political idea of prehistory was Gustaf Kossinna. His dates were 1858–1931: he began as a philologist and then turned to prehistory. In 1895 he set out his views on prehistory in a lecture at Cassel. In 1902 he was appointed Professor of German prehistory in the University of Berlin, and held this post until he died nearly thirty years later.

German interest in the German national past dates back to the same time as the first stirrings of British interest in the British past. Camden's *Britannia* was published in 1587, and at the same time the same back-looking curiosity in a new nation state was operating in Germany. In 1615 Philip Cluver (1580–1623) published a large book called *Germania Antiqua*: its aim was to assemble everything that existed in classical writers about the ancient Germans. At this time the Germans were depicted as rude barbarians and also at this time as in England and France there was little or no effort to interpret the ancient Germans from a study of their material remains. This had to wait in Germany as in England and France for the geological and antiquarian revolutions of the second quarter of the nineteenth century. Actually two Germans at this time, Danneil and Lisch, seemed to have hit on the Three Age system independently of the Danes.

The nineteenth century saw great developments in German archaeology but, at first, in the field of classical and Near-Eastern archaeology. A branch of the German Archaeological Institute was set up in Athens in 1875 and in that year excavations began at Olympia under Ernst Curtius. They occupied the six winters of 1875–80, cost £30,000, and the expenses of the last winter season were borne by the Emperor William. Later, from 1899 through to 1914 the Germans led by Koldewey and Andrae were excavating at Babylon and Ashur. These latter were most thorough and efficient excavations which revealed stratigraphic succession of occupations and effected the total clearance of town sites. Nor should we forget that Schliemann though not an official German archaeologist – and indeed himself proud of his American status – was by birth and upbringing a German; although his earlier excavations were much criticized his later work under the guidance of Dorpfeld was very good. Certainly in the last quarter of the nineteenth century the Germans were coming into their own as archaeologists.

But Kossinna complained that the new German archaeology was concentrating on classical lands and was, therefore, prepared implicitly or explicitly to describe the Germans of antiquity as poor barbarians. He complained that the Berlin Academy of Sciences welcomed representatives of Egyptian, Greek, Roman, and Oriental antiquity but no one dealing with German prehistory. He further complained that the organization of museums in Prussia made the museum of

German prehistory appear as of less importance than the collections illustrating Hottentot and Papuan life. He kept insisting that this was wrong and kept quoting the historian Sybel's doctrine that 'a nation which fails to keep in living touch with its past is as near to drying up as a tree with severed roots. We are today what we were yesterday.'

Kossinna deliberately set out to prove the importance and greatness of the Germans through prehistory. He inflated chronology so that everything seemed to have started in Germany and spread out from the superior Germans to the inferiors all around. He was quite certain about the megalith builders, for example, and had them moving out from Germany all over the ancient European and Mediterranean world. We can laugh at these fantasies of Kossinna at the present day; but he was serious about them, and they were seriously taken up by German racialists who readily accepted the apparent proof provided by prehistory of the antiquity and superiority of the Germans.

Other countries have supplied similar examples of the use of early history and prehistory for political ends. Mussolini had great illuminated maps by which the Roman Empire gradually enlarged from Rome to its fullest extent under Trajan. Then the illumination went out abruptly and, as Professor Grahame Clark remarks: 'The observer waited in vain who hoped to see unfolded successive stages in the decline and disintegration of the Empire; the lights went out abruptly and the process of growth began anew.'* And these prehistoric political tricks continue; a few years ago I saw in Madrid maps of the Iberian colonization of Europe and it was some while before I realized that I was looking at a distribution map of Beakers dating from say 2000 to 1800 B.C.

I have given you some examples of the use of a false idea of prehistory in recent politics; the best example was of course in Germany where a perversion of prehistory was crossed with

* J. G. D. Clark, *Archaeology and Society*, 1939, p. 201.

racialism and anti-semitism. The Nazi régime did not last long enough for us to have maps deriving all civilization from the Germanic north, but this might have been arranged in time. As Hitler himself said: 'There is no such thing as truth. Science is a social phenomenon and like every other social phenomenon is limited by the benefit or injury it confers on the community.'

Let us now turn briefly to Russia. Here since the revolution the possibilities of archaeology have been pursued by the N. Y. Marr Institute of Material Culture, a research organ of the Academy of Sciences of the U.S.S.R. Now one of the avowed functions of the Research Institutes of the Academy of Sciences of the U.S.S.R. is to 'organize and lead the struggle against pseudo-scientific theories and trends in the various fields of knowledge', and the late Professor A. M. Tallgren of Helsinki has told us how this struggle has disposed of the archaeologists whom he knew in the twenties. In his survey of Archaeological Studies in Soviet Russia Tallgren said sadly and cynically after giving a long list of his liquidated archaeological colleagues: 'How rich humanity must be if it can dispense with such good men.' Now, of course, these men were being disposed of so that a particular brand of prehistory could be taught in Russia, and there is no confusion or shame or uncertainty about the Russian desire to do this as there was none in Nazi Germany. Stalin himself said that the significance of historical ideas lies in the way they hamper the development and progress of society. He was saying in another way Engels's words: 'Men make their own history.' To a certain extent this is true, and my predecessor as archaeologist in giving the Josiah Mason Lectures, Gordon Childe, said roundly and frankly: 'It is just no good demanding that history shall be unbiased.'* Childe himself was praised in Soviet archaeological circles. In his The Crisis in Bourgeois Archaeology, Mongait says:

* V. G. Childe, History, 1947, p. 22.

Contemporary bourgeois archaeologists . . . are the vanguard of reaction, against which we lead and will continue to lead a bitter struggle. . . . Bourgeois archaeology, like history, is distinguished by extreme idealism (A. Goldenweiser). The English historian Collingwood goes even further . . . and Daniel follows after Taylor. . . . There are also progressive scholars who are friends of our country and who understand very well the universal significance of our science. . . . One of these is Gordon Childe; Childe has not yet succeeded in overcoming many of the errors of bourgeois science. But he understands that scientific truth is in the socialist camp and is not ashamed to call himself a pupil of Soviet archaeologists.*

We have already referred to the work of Lewis H. Morgan and how he set out a series of ethnic periods leading from Lower Savagery to Civilization. What is important at the present day is to realize that Engels was enormously influenced by Morgan. He summarized Morgan's ethnic periods in his *Origin of the Family* (1884) and there declared in a statement which of course cannot be sustained for a moment that 'Morgan is the first man who with expert knowledge has attempted to introduce a definite order into human prehistory'. At first the Russians liked the system of ethnic periods but it was not readily usable as a classification of archaeological material, and in the twenties of this century the Russians were using like everyone else the Thomsen system of the Three Ages of Stone, Bronze, and Iron. In the 1930s they abandoned this and began to speak of three grades of society, namely pre-clan society, clan society, and class society. Efimenko said that pre-clan society was represented by what we would call the Lower Palaeolithic. The rest of the Palaeolithic and the rest of prehistory was mainly clan society; first the matriarchal clans which were alleged to be Upper Palaeolithic and Mesolithic, then a transition to patriarchal clan organization beginning with the Neolithic and from then on

* Quoted from M. Miller, *Archaeology in the U.S.S.R.*, 1956, pp. 148–51.

a steady decline to class society – what was called 'the period of the disintegration of the clan'.

I want to say only two things here about all this. First that it is a deliberate going back to the psychic unity of man, to the ideas of natural, social, or supra-organic evolution. No diffusion was allowed at all. Secondly it was a hypothetical system of cultural evolution which when devised was then imposed on the archaeological material. We have seen how the first ideas of prehistory were pre-archaeological and how an archaeological idea of man's early past was developed painfully over the last hundred years. We have seen how responsible scientists like Elliot Smith rejected the idea of archaeological prehistory as unsatisfactory, and how politicians rejected prehistory based on archaeology because it did not suit their ends and replaced it by an invented prehistory based on premises like the superiority of the Germans or the natural evolution of society from pre-clan through clan to class.

I hope you are beginning to see what a great choice there is for you in ideas of prehistory. To misquote Engels, you see that men make their own prehistory. What a choice lies in front of you at present. You can have a Russian Marxist prehistory, a German chauvinist prehistory, you can have Elliot Smith and his Egyptians, or you can even bury your head in the sand and sigh for the good old days of the Phoenicians and the Druids, or, emerging from the past, pay your subscription to the Atlantis society or buy books on Tiahuanaco. Or you can, with as little prejudice as any man can bring to any problem, try to see what the prehistoric record does tell, and what at this mid-century moment we should try to evaluate as the lessons of the prehistory of man, what as historians we do now think of man's earliest history. It is to an evaluation of this task that I shall now direct your thoughts.

CHAPTER SEVEN

PREHISTORY AND THE HISTORIANS

I HAVE attempted to trace, albeit in very summary fashion, the way in which prehistory as an academic discipline and a branch of learning came into existence in the last hundred and fifty years, and to discuss the different ideas of prehistory which have been held at different times – before and after the development of archaeology as a deliberate technique of studying the material remains of the past. This development, which put an end to legendary or mythological prehistory – to prehistory based entirely on speculation – did not rule out the possibilities of prehistory which, while using archaeological methods like distribution maps and the comparative study of material remains, yet flourished with such a disregard for facts as virtually to revert to mythology and to the days of pre-archaeological prehistory.

I now want to consider what has, in fact, been created by a century and a half of archaeological investigation and prehistorical research. In the first place a branch of learning, an academic discipline, has been brought into existence and one which, as we shall discuss in the last lecture, has at the moment great and surprisingly great claims on the interest of the general public. What is this branch of learning? What does it try to tell us? What does it tell us? What are its relationships to kindred fields of study like human geography, sociology, anthropology, history? And what is the relevance of its teachings, its conclusions, its perspective of the past to us as private individuals, as political individuals, and as educationists? These are some of the questions about the nature and relevance of the idea of prehistory that I am now proposing to discuss.

First, of course, a word about the eternal question which

besets everyone who sets out to discuss the nature of any branch of learning; is it a science or not? In the end it is all a matter not of absolute values and ultimate decisions but of terminology and definitions. We ourselves have made these terms science, the humanities, the arts, the human sciences, and whether a new branch of learning which we as scholars have created, developed, and defined, falls within any of these terms depends on how we define them – how we define them now and how we have defined them in the past.

Originally science meant all knowledge and in the seventeenth century when the Royal Society (which we nowadays regard as the stronghold of science) came into existence it comprised all knowledge. It certainly dealt not only with what we should now call the natural sciences but with the material remains of man, and in its early days counted as members men like John Aubrey and Edward Lhuyd, who were antiquaries. Yet they were polymaths and Lhuyd himself wrote about asbestos and fossils as well as about New Grange and Cornish and Breton. And there was nothing odd in the early days of the Royal Society in a Fellow of my own College in Cambridge, Martin Lister, reading papers to the Royal Society both on zoology and on Roman remains. A liberal polymathy comprised all these interests. Aubrey, Lhuyd, Lister did not call themselves scientists.

When Sir Isaac Newton became president of the Royal Society he discouraged an interest in the material remains of the past and the Royal Society began to confine its interests to what we now call the natural sciences, to the study of nature and to exclude the study of man's culture. Here began or was first formalized the distinction between the study of nature and the study of man – between the sciences and the arts, or between the natural sciences and the human sciences. The arts or humanities, by definition, deal with man as a cultured animal, in fact the only animal with culture, with a transmittable body of ideas, customs, beliefs, and practices dependent on that main agent of transmission, language, and in the last few millennia of his existence, that other main agent of cultural transmission, the written word.

It is beyond dispute that by practice in school examination and university degree system and in general parlance we distinguish between the natural sciences (or the natural and physical sciences) and the humanities (or the arts or the human sciences). It is also beyond dispute that this distinction is not only one of subject-matter but of fundamental principles; the natural scientist hopes to find laws which are immutable and which are indeed the ultimate facts of the natural world. The scholar who devotes himself to man and his works may hope, and may piously declare that he aims, to find laws of a similar nature. But this he never does unless general statements, like 'Man is a religious animal', or 'Man is a historic animal' (meaning that no known societies exist in which there is no religion and no awareness of the past), are thought to be general laws.

There are then two customary ways of using the word science; it can mean knowledge or it can mean knowledge of nature. There is of course a third way in which we use the word science or particularly the adjective 'scientific'. That is as applied to method. We speak of the scientific method when we mean the use of principles of collecting evidence, deduction, experimentation – but these have by now become so much a general part of the methodical exploration of all knowledge that we sometimes find people thinking the scientific method is no more than just common sense.

When, then, we are asked, 'Is prehistory a science?' we are really being asked one of three questions, namely, 'Is prehistory a part of knowledge?' and 'Is prehistory concerned with nature?' and 'Is prehistory scientific in its method?' The answer to the first and third questions is in the affirmative, but to the second the answer must surely be no. Prehistory deals with man and not with nature and is not part of the natural sciences: it is part of human not natural history. It comes, of course, very close to the natural sciences and indeed is the bridge between geology and history. It deals a great deal with periods of time, the Pleistocene and Holocene, which are the concern of the geologist and natural historian, and uses a great number of techniques which belong to the natural and physical sciences such as Carbon-14 analysis, fluorine analysis, the petrological analysis of stone, the metallurgical analysis of metals, to mention only a few of these analytical techniques.

The prehistorian is dependent for a great deal of his information about the biome of early man,* the vegetation in which a society flourished, the plants they collected or grew, the animals they hunted or reared, on expert advice from zoologists and botanists; and it is a prerequisite of the training of a prehistorian, more especially if he is going to concern himself with the long millennia of human development comprised by the terms Palaeolithic and Mesolithic, that he should be thoroughly grounded in the natural sciences which serve him. It is also true that in dealing with the Lower Palaeolithic cultures the prehistorian is little different from the Pleistocene geologist who is studying the fossils of horse or hippo in the same deposits. The cultural fossils may appear little different from the organic fossils in the technique required for their discovery and study. But Acheulian hand axes are cultural fossils and the product of the human mind and human craftsmanship. The scholar who studies Neanderthal man's bones is a natural scientist while he who studies Neanderthal man's artifacts is a historian, however little cultural material he has to work on. This break in the study of man grows as the complexity of the archaeological evidence grows. We would not today confuse the specialist who studies our bones with the

* This useful but inelegant phrase was coined by J. G. D. Clark in his *Prehistoric Europe: The Economic Basis*, Cambridge, 1950. It is no accident that the Chair of Archaeology concerned with the Palaeolithic and Mesolithic in the University of London is called the Professorship of Environmental Archaeology.

man who studies our crafts or culture. We should not make this confusion in prehistory because in the very remote past the cultural and the physical records are so thin and one scholar can be master of both. Prehistory is then a humanity; it is the earliest phase of historical study. It is part of history and those who would call it science are using the word science in a very special way. Prehistory is part of human history and, therefore, suffers from all the problems inherent in historical method – the difficulty of evaluating evidence, the inability of writing without some form of bias, and the constantly changing picture of history according to the changing ways and ideas and preconceptions of historians.

But it suffers from far more difficulties than those which beset the writer of history, difficulties based mainly or entirely on written records. The main difficulty is that by definition prehistoric archaeology is dealing with pre-written sources only; so that all prehistory is anonymous. We do not know the name of the architect of Stonehenge, or of the man whose body was recovered from the Tollund peat-bog in Jutland and whose noble features look calmly at us across twenty centuries. We do not know the names of the communities or societies whose material culture we study and classify as cultures. This is why prehistory reads with such difficulty to so many people, with its Beaker people and its Long Barrow men, not to say its pieces of archaeological algebra like Iron Age I (a) i. And the difference between pre-written and written history goes much deeper than names and the absence of names. It is this more fundamental fact that from pre-literate sources we know and can know only a part of the total culture of these pre-literate societies. Prehistory not only deals with anonymous societies grouped into divisions of its own devising; but it is inevitably mainly concerned with the material cultural aspects of these anonymous societies. This is, as I have said, inevitable from the nature of the archaeological source, for what survive from prehistoric times are stone tools, bronze weapons, hut foundations, tombs, field walls, and the like. We are accustomed to speak of the imperishable ideals of a society, but the prehistorian is witness to the sad fact that the ideals perish, and it is the cutlery and chinaware of a society that are imperishable. We have no way of learning the moral and religious ideas of the protohistoric city dwellers of Mohenjo-Daro and Harappa but their drains, their brick rubbish chutes, and their terracotta toys survive.

It is in the fact that the prehistorian seems to be concerned mainly with varieties of houses and tombs and cutlery and safety pins that many have found the greatest criticism of the subject. Prehistory would appear to be concerned, some have argued, with the non-essentials of human life: 'We do not wish to know,' say these critics, 'about the types of safety pin used by the Early Iron Age farmers of France, or the details of tomb construction adopted by the metal prospectors of 2000 B.C. in western Europe; we want to know the essentials of these societies – how they lived, what they thought, what were their ideals and illusions.'

Now there is some truth and much distortion in this view of prehistory. Prehistory is not concerned only with types of safety pins and tombs; it uses these and other facts to build up a picture of prehistoric life – how food was obtained, what sort of villages and farms existed, what were the crops and field systems and animals, what were the types of burial custom. Certainly prehistory concerns itself with the types of life of prehistoric societies. But equally certainly it does not speak about the spiritual, mental, and moral culture of these societies. It cannot speak of the social organization or the religious beliefs of prehistoric society, and this is a fundamental limitation of prehistory. When prehistorians speak of the ideas and ideals of men before writing, they are making guesses – intelligent guesses by people best qualified to make them, but nevertheless guesses.

Some prehistorians have attempted to break through this

limiting factor by using two methods of special, and to my mind doubtful, validity. The first is the use of ethnographical comparisons, and the second is the acceptance as fact of hypothetical evolutionary systems. Let us discuss the use of ethnographical parallels first. Balked by the absence of detail in prehistory, or so it must seem as one looks at the limitations and intractability of the surviving archaeological material, some prehistorians have turned to surviving pre-literate societies, namely the present-day primitive societies studied by the anthropologist, which only just miss being classified as prehistory. The archaeologists seek in these existing societies a guide to the way of life of our prehistoric ancestors. A good example of this is provided by W. J. Sollas in his *Ancient Hunters*, first published in 1911.

To a certain extent the use of these ethnographical parallels is fair and just. The prehistorian can understand the nature of the prehistoric artifacts he studies only by comparing them with those used by modern primitives. But some prehistorians, not content with inferring the function of prehistoric artifacts from the identity of form between prehistoric and modern artifacts, have gone further and have assumed that the identity of form between the artifacts of modern pre-literates and of prehistoric societies means not only probable identity of function in material culture, but also identity in the social structure and mental and spiritual beliefs of the two societies being compared. Surely this assumption is most fallacious because the Magdalenian folk of south France have certain parallels in formal material culture with the Eskimo, we cannot argue that they have the same economic organization, marriage customs, or beliefs about the after-life. It is not even reasonably probable that the same form of artifact should imply the same kind of economic organization, let alone social structure, or mental and spiritual culture; and this inherent improbability is borne in on one the more one studies the variety of social and mental culture that exists at the present day among the so-called primitive communities of the world. In short, as Ehrenburg has put it, 'it is a delusion to think that "experimenting" with the so-called primitives of yesterday and today provides scientific material for prehistory and history'.

I am not saying that by trying to understand the life of the Tlingit and Haida in British Columbia, for example, or of the Bushman Hunters of South Africa, one does not get a better view of the inside of food-gathering communities in the past than if one confines one's viewpoint to modern twentieth century food-producing cultures in southern England; nor am I saying that the technology and spiritual life of pre-literate societies do not give us hints and suggestions of great value in the interpretation of prehistoric artifacts. The same is true of the study of modern folk cultures as Professor Grahame Clark has often insisted, but again it gives only suggestions and hints, and cannot be used deterministically.* Ethnographic determinism is as dangerous as any other determinist doctrine; we cannot say, for example, that because the Tasmanians when they were discovered, described, and destroyed in the nineteenth century were formally Neolithic, that they are a complete guide to the ideas and beliefs of all Neolithic communities. And the same is very true of the food-gathering communities which in a general way we can compare with the Palaeolithic and Mesolithic hunting–fishing communities. Indeed there is a tremendous variety among the beliefs of hunting communities; compare the rich and leisurely British Columbians with their *potlatch* economy and their fine woodwork and blankets on the one hand and the Tasmanians on the other – both are formally Neolithic.

The real point here is that, quite apart from our present problem, there is no coincidence between the material and

* J. G. D. Clark, 'Folk-culture and the study of European prehistory' in (Ed.) W. F. Grimes, *Aspects of Archaeology in Britain and Beyond*, 1951, p. 49, and *Prehistoric Europe: The Economic Basis*, 1952, and *Archaeology and Society*, third edition, 1957.

non-material aspects of culture. Indeed why should there be? And if we once accept this, it is clearly useless to expect the moral and mental culture of modern primitives in the same or apparently the same state of material culture as some prehistoric primitives, to give us a real or true guide to the moral and mental culture of the prehistoric society.

If ethnography does not help us in reconstructing the total picture of prehistoric societies, what can we turn to? I have already referred to the evolutionary systems of cultural development which were being proposed in the nineteenth century. Spencer, Tylor, and Jevons suggested stages in the supposed religious evolution of man, while Bachofen, McLennan, and Morgan suggested stages of social evolution. I have already spoken of Morgan's ethnic stages and how they were approved of by Engels and how Marxism has made use of these fallacious evolutionary systems. The interesting thing, for our immediate purpose, is that some prehistorians have accepted these evolutionary sequences as of equal validity with the sequence of technological stages associated with Thomsen and it is from these equations that we find the Neolithic Age being spoken of as one of primitive communism, the Bronze Age as seeing the beginnings of private property, and so on. Now all this is a process of hypostasization; of treating proposed evolutionary sequences as facts, and of forgetting that all the nineteenth-century cultural evolutionary sequences, like the sequence proposed by Soviet archaeologists for pre-clan, clan, and class society, are merely schemes, ideas, and projects. They may be right, but they are invalid as a source for the mental and spiritual life of prehistoric man – as invalid, though as suggestive, as our ethnographical parallels.

But there is this difference between ethnographical parallels and hypothetical systems. The facts of the ethnographical parallels are accurate; it is merely using them as deterministic parallels that is wrong. But the facts of the supposed evolutionary cultural sequences of man are not necessarily facts at all; these sequences are mainly the result of nineteenth-century evolutionary thought and a belief that cultural or supra-organic evolution must necessarily follow physical evolution, and which arranged all social and cultural phenomena in such sequences. It is easy to set out baldly the basis of this nine-teenth-century thought: monogamy and monotheism were the practices and the virtues of the nineteenth century, and the extremes from these practices, namely polygamy or promis-cuity and animism, were necessarily what the earliest men thought and practised. Of course, subsequent anthropological work has shown that many of these alleged early stages in belief and practice just do not exist, and that their arrangement in sequences is pure hypothesis.

We are then driven back from modern primitives and the schemes of historical anthropologists to the hard archaeo-logical facts. How hard are they, and how exciting can we make our modern story of ancient man? We must repeat that our only source for information on prehistoric times is archaeology. In the Josiah Mason Lectures which Professor Gordon Childe gave in Birmingham in 1947-8, and which were published in his book *Social Evolution* in 1951, he asked how far it was legitimate to infer non-material facts about pre-historic man from the material remains that survive. I do not want to go over the ground he trod so well in dealing with this question, but let us put the question in its crudest form in front of ourselves like this. When we look at the great paint-ings in the hillside of Lascaux are we really able to say that they were done for purposes of sympathetic hunting magic? When we see the great stone tombs in France with their carved goddess figures, can we say that these are the tombs of chieftains who imposed their beliefs on an impoverished pop-ulation? When we find two people, a man and a woman, buried in the same grave, does it mean suttee or murder, or that they both died at the same time through some disease? Let us look at this archaeological problem in a different way.

If one day – which God forbid – my own University City of Cambridge is reduced to uninhabited ruins, and no written records survive of its life, the ruins will show several rectangular buildings like King's College Chapel, many cinemas, the Examination Schools, and public buildings like the Corn Exchange which is nowadays used mainly as a skating rink. The archaeologist of the future, if he has no written or epigraphical sources, will surely lump together all these rectangular buildings as 'public ritual buildings', and, in a way, so they are whether they be College chapel, skating rink, or cinema. One thing will puzzle the archaeologist and that is the ruins of the Church of St Sepulchre, one of the four round churches of Britain. This too would clearly be a ritual or cult building; it is obviously not a tomb or a house. Perhaps the archaeologist of the future would distinguish two cultures in Cambridge, one having long rectangular buildings and the other having round buildings. Within the justifiable limits of exaggeration to emphasize a point, this is just the sort of way, uncritically, that archaeologists might work.

Now let us look at Gordon Childe's conclusions. Here are his words:

In certain circumstances, and always with reserve, archaeology can provide some indications as to the form of government and of the family, the recognition of rank, the distribution of the social product and the practice of war. It is never likely to be able to tell us anything about the administration of justice, the penalties needed to enforce it, nor the contents of any laws, the way in which descent rather than the inheritance of property is determined, the effective limitations on the powers of chiefs, or even of the extent of their authority. The content of religious belief and the nature of the prestige conferred by rank are irretrievably lost.[*]

I have deliberately quoted at length these words by one of our most distinguished prehistorians whose mind was so agile

[*] V. G. Childe, *Social Evolution*, 1951, p. 55.

and nimble that he took an almost perverse delight in archaeological experimentation – in turning upside down theories
which the orthodox (including himself of a few weeks or
months or years ago) taught and wrote about. He himself in
his *Scotland Before the Scots*, admittedly a wicked experiment
in archaeological interpretation, did not practise the reserva-
tions which he laid down in his Mason lectures.* These reser-
vations are right ones, and it follows from our acceptance of
them that not only is the record of the prehistoric past limited,
not only can we not answer so many of the questions which
the interested public ask, but also that it is impossible to equate
any of the theoretical stages of cultural evolution with archaeological stages. Let me say one thing about this again: when I
spoke of the work of the Russians and the application of
archaeology to their schemes of pre-clan, clan, and class
society, I did not mean that the schemes were necessarily
wrong; merely that it was wrong to pretend that the record
of prehistoric archaeology proved these schemes. The unfortunate fact that must be faced is that prehistoric archaeology
does not tell us so much of what we want to know as historians
of man about man's early life.

And here perhaps we come to the very nub of an extremely
important and interesting problem. Why do historians in a
general way pay so little attention to this fourth division of
the study of the human past; while recognizing ancient history
do they not give more recognition to prehistory? Just take a
look at any of our short histories of this country from Trevelyan through Feiling and Arthur Bryant to Winston Churchill;
in all of them all we get about pre-Roman Britain is a short
curtain-raiser and we are moved hurriedly and with relief on
to the Romans with their names and dates and inscriptions and
good historical habits. Let me quote the words at the end of

* Childe was alive at the time I gave the Mason lectures in Birmingham.
He died in October 1957.

George Trevelyan's introduction to the beginnings of British history:

The study of the Mingling of the Races in Britain, ending with the advent of the Normans, covers a thousand years of history very dimly descried, succeeding to many thousands more of archaeological twilight. The era of Celt, Saxon, and Dane is like Macbeth's battle on the blasted heath. Prophecy hovers around. Horns are heard blowing in the mist, and a confused uproar of savage tumult and outrage. We catch glimpses of giant figures – mostly warriors at strife. But there are ploughmen, too, it seems, breaking the primeval clod, and we hear the sounds of forests crashing to the axe. Around all is the lap of waves and the cry of seamen beaching their ships.

These words were originally written in 1926 but they are still relevant. Historians are taking a long time to integrate prehistory into their general view of man. There are many reasons for this. First the material of prehistory is, as we have seen, difficult and different. Secondly, it is often tantalizingly inadequate and refuses to provide the answers to so many problems we ask. In the third place, I think many historians are still suspicious of some of the preoccupations and ideas of prehistoric archaeologists.

It has seemed to me that one of the reasons why prehistory was not more immediately accepted by historians as part of their general story was that the prehistoric archaeologists were sometimes, in the last thirty years or so, apparently suspect because of their association with geographers. I mean here nothing, of course, rude or derogatory about geographers, nor that the geographer has not a role and function in the study of prehistory. Indeed the geographer has very important, interesting, and vital roles. There are endless definitions of the scope and nature of geography – almost as many as there are Professors of Geography – but what everyone is agreed about is that the geographer in the modern convenient arrangement of fields of study is concerned with the face of the earth, and is perhaps at his finest when he is describing small areas of the earth's surface, when he is engaged in regional geography. Here the geographer is doing what the good historian does when he takes a small period of time in an area and tells us all he can about the historical context of the space–time area so defined. Similarly the geographer is at his best in giving us geographical contexts; he tells us for example what the face of Brittany looks like and describes the features on that rugged sea-girt countenance – the mountains and rivers, the driving rains and thick sea-mists, the harbours and the sardine and tunny fisheries, the isolated granite farmsteads, the long cold meadows. In any geographical context there are natural and cultural features to the landscape, and if we analyse the cultural landscape we will find that it is of two kinds – the living and functional cultural landscape, and the dead, fossil, cultural landscape. The geographer, as he describes his region or chosen area, as he analyses the man-made features of the face of the earth and constructs his geographical context, is constantly coming up against the dead and the dying – prehistoric earthworks, Roman villas, Norman *mottes*, dead and decaying towns, deserted villages, nineteenth-century disused railways. All these things he sees as he sees the living towns and villages and farms and factories of the landscape. The geographer then shares the non-functional cultural landscape with the archaeologist and the barrows and banks and ditches of pre-Roman Britain are as much his concern in one way as they are the concern of the prehistorian in another.

We surely do not need to labour this point, but let us take just one example: Dartmoor. The geography of Dartmoor must most necessarily be concerned with the dead aspects of the landscape – the cultural fossils of the period generally referred to as from the Early Bronze Age through to the Roman Conquest – a period of some fifteen hundred years from which survive stone rows and circles, megalithic tombs, field pounds, huts, and smelting sites. The geographer must needs know about all this if he is ever to read accurately the face of Dartmoor, and so must the prehistorian if he is trying to reconstruct historical contexts and understand why and how people lived on the moor in the pre-Roman centuries. The geographer and the prehistorian meet in the map. Prehistory is vitally concerned with the distribution of the material remains which survive from the prehistoric past; indeed this is the first of its two techniques of interpretation – examining an antiquity or a culture in space and time. Space means the map and the distribution map has been a key feature of archaeological interpretation, research, and exposition for over sixty to seventy years.

But the geographer does not study one element of the cultural landscape alone: he sees it as part of the total landscape made up of natural and cultural features. Very gradually this geographical approach to prehistory became popular. Antiquities and cultures were studied not merely distributionally on a blank map of Europe but geographically on a map of soils, rocks, climate, and vegetation and in relation to these facts of physical geography. The German geologist Gradmann did this in 1898 and as a result argued that prehistoric settlement was virtually confined to open country – country of a steppe-like character – and this of course included the loess lands. In England O. G. S. Crawford began preparing maps of antiquities and studying them against the background of prehistoric vegetation, or, rather, the postulated background of prehistoric vegetation; his maps of *Neolithic Wessex* and *Roman Britain* are perhaps the best-known examples of this work.

In 1916 two geographers working at the University College of Wales, Aberystwyth, namely H. J. Fleure and W. E. Whitehouse, argued that from distributional studies alone one could say that prehistoric man lived on the hill-tops and only gradually moved down into the valley bottoms. Of course there is some truth in this. We know how in the early period of Roman occupation the conquered Ancient Britons moved from hill-forts like St Catharine's Hill and Maiden Castle to lowland settlements like Winchester and Dorchester. But Fleure and Whitehouse made this a general law: the law of the Early Valleyward Movement of Population in Southern Britain, and as a general law it began to look dangerous, and deterministic, and unhistorical. In 1923 Sir Cyril Fox published his *Archaeology of the Cambridge Region* and showed how the pattern of settlement had changed in relation to the natural vegetation; he was able to show that what Fleure and Whitehouse had observed in Wales was a specialized instance of the real trends in British prehistory, namely the shift from primary to secondary areas of settlement, from light easily worked soils to the hard, difficult, waterlogged clayey soils; that it was a Welsh mountain version of a general principle. Indeed, Mortimer Wheeler has cynically described the work of the Aberystwyth geographers as a doctrine 'naturally popularized by a school of able and eloquent geographers working in a mountain environment'.*

Following on his studies in East Anglia, Fox tested his thesis in relation to England and Wales as a whole and we see his ideas set out in *The Personality of Britain*, first published in 1932. Here Fox combined the ecological–distributional ideas of people like Gradmann and Crawford with the ideas of positional geography developed by Halford Mackinder in his *Britain and the British Seas* and the 'personality' idea of the French geographers. But it began to savour rather strangely of geographical determinism; prehistorians and historians began to get suspicious. They began to get more suspicious when other prehistorians referred to Fox's interesting and suggestive conclusions as 'Fox's laws'. In the revised fourth edition of *The Personality of Britain* he says, 'The further a continental society is from the Mediterranean the more barbarous it will be,' and confesses that he was driven to study the geographical factor in prehistory because he was looking for a unifying

* R. E. M. Wheeler, *Prehistoric and Roman Wales*, 1925, p. 214.

force to take the place in pre-literate days of the individual factor in historical days.

But should we assume that the geographical factor is any more powerful among pre-literate societies in the prehistoric past than it is in historic times; should we underestimate the personal factor in prehistory just because the persons are nameless? I do not want to take up any more space here in discussing the validity of the ideas of geographical determinism in prehistory: most people today would say that there were no mandatory geographical laws in prehistory, as in history, except the obvious extreme mandates of climate and natural resources. These when stated baldly are obvious platitudes – it is clear that the climate and resources in the South and North poles have not made those areas centres of population and cradles of civilization. It is equally obvious that a bronze industry cannot originate and flourish naturally or easily in an area where copper and tin do not exist. My concern here is to suggest that these geographical ideas of prehistory arose and flourished for a while and did something to make prehistory suspect to the formal historians; it became to some of them for a while something like historical geography, emphasizing a facile and inaccurate explanation of a series of facts which might not be explicable at all. The historians then, in their approach to prehistory, have had to get over their dislike of the geographical determinist bias.

They have also had to get over their intrinsic dislike of the over-advocacy of the importance of prehistoric archaeology, of the school of scholars who said in all good faith that a sherd of decorated pottery was worth all Herodotus, or that 'to the peoples of the world generally . . . Palaeolithic man has more meaning than the Greeks'.* They have also had to get over the way in which men trained in the methods and results of prehistory have extended their studies to include the whole of history and produced books which seemed to put the study

* J. G. D. Clark, *Antiquity*, 1943, p. 118.

of written history into an unimportant position *vis-à-vis* pre-history. Admittedly, as the American anthropologist Lowie has said, written history is 'only the final scene of a lengthy drama', and it is surely impossible for thinking people today to study history by studying only written history; that would be, as Charles Letourneau said half a century ago, like trying 'to reconstruct a book from its last chapter'. But a prehistorian like Gordon Childe goes too far in the opposite direction when he calls a book that deals mainly with prehistory and protohistory, *What Happened in History* and we see the same sort of problem though not in such a degree in Carleton S. Coon's *The History of Man*.

Nevertheless books such as these and the writing of pre-history as a whole have done a great deal to jerk modern historians into a new universalist outlook. World or Universal History existed in the sixteenth century, but it gradually be-came more and more specialized and detailed, particularly since 1881 when Pope Leo XIII opened the Vatican archives and, in England, since 1886, when Sir Henry Maxwell Lyte became Director of the Public Record Office. A new and de-tailed form of history developed, sharply described by Geoffrey Barraclough as 'that devoted worship and admiring contemplation of its own navel which has made many other-wise not unsympathetic observers ask whether the measurable results justified the immeasurable expenditure of effort'.* Whether this be true or not, we must agree with Butterfield when he says that 'Universal history has ceased to hold a prominent place in our interests presumably because it spreads the mind over so wide an area that the knowledge can hardly avoid becoming too thin'.†

I shall comment again on the view that the knowledge becomes too thin; here let me underline the phrase 'spreads the mind'. Is that not really what we want historians and

---

* G. Barraclough, *History in a Changing World*, 1956, p. 16.
† H. Butterfield, *Man on his Past*, 1955, p. 44.

prehistorians to do as well as to concentrate on the intricacies of nineteenth-century Germany or the construction of Stonehenge, and is not that why we welcome H. G. Wells's *Outline of History*, Gordon Childe's *What Happened in History*, and Coon's *The History of Man* even if we criticize them in detail? Here is the broad sweep which we need. To quote Barraclough again:

> The crying need today is not for specialization, which means fragmentation, but for integration and this requires not simply specialized knowledge but the general historical understanding of the course of European and indeed extra-European history.*

There has been one historian in the last fifteen years who has revived universal history and tried to make historians look at the world other than as a western European world. I refer to Professor Arnold J. Toynbee, but his conclusions and his basic thesis do not recommend themselves to a prehistorian. His basic thesis, as I understand it, is that we can distinguish a certain number of complicated societies which he calls civilizations with their cities, technologies, and religions, and that we can study them in isolation from their past and their contemporary civilizations and we can see them behaving as living organisms.

Let us look very briefly at Toynbee in relation to the problem usually referred to as that of the birth of civilization. Archaeological research has shown that the earliest traces of civilization – that is to say societies with writing and a city life – are found in Egypt, Palestine, and Mesopotamia. We know now that writing, urban life, and the arts of metallurgy were invented in one centre or in several centres in what Breasted called the Fertile Crescent. Now, of course, it is vital to Toynbee's thesis to study the origin of the oldest of his civilizations in the Near East. This he does and these are his conclusions: he attributes the origin of civilization to the

* G. Barraclough, op. cit., p. 20.

desiccation of the Sahara and represents this desiccation as a challenge to be overcome. He makes the valleys of the Nile and the Tigris–Euphrates not delectable as do the geographical prehistorians like Peake and Fleure, but horrible jungle swamps – another challenge to be overcome. Toynbee then says that six things happened to man as the Sahara dried up and became a desert: first, some people stayed there and perished; secondly some people stayed where they were in the Sahara, mastered the challenge of the environment, and evolved a nomadic way of life; thirdly some went south and retained their old way of life, becoming the Dinka and Shilluk. In the fourth place some people went north, according to Toynbee, and became the Neolithic agriculturists of the European continent – although Toynbee does not tell us how these folk discovered agriculture on the way along a route where cereals do not occur wild. Fifthly there were those who plunged into the jungle swamps of the Near East and met this challenge by inventing civilization: and sixth and last there were those who plunged across the sea and made the Minoan civilization.

The real tragedy of Toynbee's writing on the origin of civilization is that here is a distinguished historian with a flair for universal history who has somehow failed to understand the archaeological record. Instead of using his great gifts towards the acquisition and synthesis of knowledge to provide us with the universal history we so much want in the middle of the twentieth century, he has confused the early history of man with his predetermined patterns, and has, therefore, further discredited universal history and the study of prehistory in the eyes of specialist historians.

In concluding our discussion on these matters I must make two confessions. First, prehistorians have been until recently rather loath to popularize their work. The lead given by Lubbock's *Prehistoric Times* in 1865 has not been followed until very recently. You may find this a strange statement of mine and may think that the railway bookstalls disprove it any day. It is true that there are books on how the archaeologist works and the method and limitations of prehistory, but, to the best of my knowledge, there does not exist a book setting out impartially, authoritatively, and simply the prehistory of Europe. We still await a good book telling the public what went on in Europe before the Roman conquest and while such a gap exists in the literature how can one blame the Toynbees of the world for displaying in prehistoric matters an abysmal ignorance which a first-year undergraduate reading Archaeology and Anthropology would get rid of in the Michaelmas Term?

Secondly, prehistory is only now in the last ten years becoming consciously a historical discipline and realizing that its job is writing history and not classifying antiques. We have a great backlog of scholarship to make up here because the excavators and museum curators still naturally tend to think that the work of archaeology is virtually over when they have dealt with it. There is, to my mind, a great danger here – the danger of a new antiquarianism in archaeology. I am not in any way decrying excavation which is the surgery of the fossil landscape and the essential prerequisite of any archaeology, nor museums which are the Public Record Office of the prehistorian. But I am saying that we too often pay lip service to prehistoric archaeology and declare it to be the discipline of writing history from archaeology, without perhaps writing any history ourselves. The description of artifacts was one stage in the development of prehistory: the description of cultures was a second. A quarter of a century ago we could have Grahame Clark saying that 'the science of archaeology might well be defined as the study of the past distribution of culture traits in time and space', and Gordon Childe defining the task of prehistory as 'largely devoted to isolating . . . cultural groups of people tracing their differentiations, wanderings and activities'. These were true statements but prehistory was then still in a stage on the way to the historical study of prehistorical times. In his *A Study of Archaeology*, W. W. Taylor urges that the prehistorian is not concerned with listing cultures but in studying culture, not in delimiting regional variations of little importance within a historical context but in studying the context as a whole. As Brøndsted has said, 'the goal of archaeology is the history of culture'.

And to that goal we now move slowly and surely. A really notable stage in that movement is represented by Grahame Clark's *Prehistoric Europe: The Economic Basis*. In this book the individual and unimportant varieties of material culture are gone; gone too is the microtomic specialization of industry and culture. Here we are looking at the development of man's economic life in prehistoric Europe portrayed on a broad canvas. Here, at last, is prehistory as the historians – or at least the economic historians – understand it. And here at last is one pattern of the future of prehistory.

CHAPTER EIGHT

PREHISTORY AND THE PUBLIC

IN *The Times* of London for 19 July 1956 there appeared a curious little paragraph amusingly headed by an intelligent sub-editor, 'Judicial Archaeology'. This is what the paragraph said:

During the hearing in the Chancery Division at the Royal Courts of Justice of a war damage case concerned with buildings in the City of London, Mr Justice Vaisey told Mr Harold Williams, Q.C. 'There is nothing more interesting than the investigation of the history of old sites. This very building in which we are now sitting was built on the site of a very old farm, and the actual site of the well which was used for watering the cattle is in the building.'

The report did not tell us any more – what Mr Williams said in reply, nor is it relevant to our present purpose. What is relevant and interesting here is Mr Justice Vaisey's first sentence: 'There is nothing more interesting than the investigation of the history of old sites.' You must admit that this is a forthright and sweeping declaration.

A few days before I read this rather unusual report in *The Times* I had been reading a review in the *Antiquaries Journal** by my Cambridge colleague Miles C. Burkitt who had been teaching prehistory in Cambridge for over thirty years and who in 1921 produced the first book in the English language to be called *Prehistory* – some seventy years after Daniel Wilson first used that word. In this review Mr Burkitt said 'Prehistory at present is popular,'* and we cannot disagree with this brief alliterative doctrine. I have had for some while a close connexion with archaeological broadcasting, and from

* M. C. Burkitt, *Antiquaries Journal*, 1956, p. 96.

the existence and continuance of archaeological programmes on sound radio and TV, from the large audiences they attract, from the most extensive and interesting correspondence they promote, it is abundantly clear that prehistory *is* popular at present, that the public likes prehistory, wants prehistory, and often prefers prehistoric archaeology to many other subjects. Indeed in an unguarded moment recently at a College Feast in Cambridge I heard Sir Ian Jacob, then Director-General of the B.B.C., say that the two popular things on television seemed to be archaeology and show-jumping.

You will all have heard of the German Marek who writes under the pseudonym C. W. Ceram and the success of whose book *Gods, Graves and Scholars* is by itself a proof of the widespread popularity of prehistoric archaeology. In his second book, translated into English under the title of *Narrow Pass, Black Mountain*, Ceram says: 'The British were, and are, fascinated by archaeological questions as are no other people in Europe';* and the number of books on archaeology pouring from our presses surely emphasizes this point of view.

Here surely is a curious state of affairs and it is worth analysing and discussing. Why is prehistory, which was not in existence as an organized discipline or a branch of learning a hundred years ago, a popular subject today? Is it due, as some have said, kindly or unkindly according to how you interpret their remarks and the adjectives they choose, to the existence of a small group of people who have found it easy and amusing and profitable to put archaeology across by the means which success in this great new educational and entertainment medium of television apparently demands, namely panel games, documentary films, personality promotion? There is some truth in this and I would be guilty of a very false modesty if I tried to deny that sound programmes like *The Archaeologist*, and television programmes like *Animal, Vegetable, Mineral?* and *Buried Treasure*, had not contributed a great deal to the

---

* C. W. Ceram, *Narrow Pass, Black Mountain*, 1956, p. 21.

present popularity of prehistory. But the interest was there before: the agencies of mass communication like sound and visual radio have, as I believe they can do with any branch of learning, widened the audience in quality and multiplied it enormously in size; but archaeology was an attraction and prehistory was popular long before Marconi invented the wireless and Sir George Barnes the Third Programme.

In the year [1956] when Penguin Books celebrated their twenty-first anniversary we tended to think that popular education was a very recent thing; but this is not so. The British Association for the Advancement of Science was founded in 1830–1 and its primary and principal purpose was the dissemination in the widest possible way of scientific knowledge. In 1851, at its Ipswich meeting, it admitted Ethnology as a distinct section, and during the period 1840–70 many contributions on prehistoric archaeology appeared in the Geology and Ethnology sections.

Thirty years before the foundation of the British Association, George Birkbeck of Glasgow had started the first course of lectures which developed into the first Mechanics' Institute. The London Mechanics' Institute was founded by Birkbeck and Brougham in 1826 and in the second quarter of the nineteenth century these Mechanics' Institutes were very important in disseminating knowledge to the lower middle classes. G. M. Young has argued that the work of the Society for the Diffusion of Useful Knowledge and the Literary, Scientific, and Mechanics' Institutes was mainly literary, and was concerned with, for example, the Bible and its commentaries, Milton, the economists, philosophers, and historians: science, he said, apart from phrenology, 'for want of apparatus, did not much affect the workman: the culture of the self-educated man was still literary'.*

This may be true of physical science, but geology and the geological beginnings of archaeology were certainly finding

* G. M. Young, *Victorian England*, 1936, p. 74.

their place in the work of these institutes. Let us take William Pengelly as an example. Pengelly was a private tutor at Torquay who was fascinated by archaeology; he had an overmastering passion for geological research. He explored Kent's Cavern in 1846 under the auspices of the Torquay Natural History Society, and later under the British Association for the Advancement of Science. He superintended the excavations at Windmill Hill, Brixham from 1858 to 1859 which convinced many people of the authenticity of the antiquity of man. He himself, as well as being an original worker, was most keen on popularizing his finds and his first success as an expositor was in the Torquay Mechanics' Institute. Wherever Pengelly lectured, whether to the Mechanics' Institute at Torquay, or to the Sciences Lecture Association in Glasgow, and on whatever subject – Kent's Cavern, the discoveries on the Somme, the caves at Mentone – his audiences were large and enthusiastic.

The *Encyclopaedia Britannica* first appeared (in three volumes) between 1768 and 1771 in Edinburgh; and the *Chambers's Encyclopaedia* (completed in 1868) by the Edinburgh firm of W. R. Chambers who had already published *Chambers's Journal* since 1832, the *Educational Course*, and the *Miscellany of Instructive and Amusing Tracts* begun in 1845 and completed in twenty volumes 'to furnish innocent entertainment mingled with correct information and instruction'. In 1844 Robert Chambers's *Vestiges of Creation* had been published anonymously; in its way it was comparable to Wells's *Outline of History* published in 1920 and Carleton Coon's *The History of Man* published in 1955. Special mention should be made here of T. D. Fosbrook's *Encyclopaedia of Antiquities and Elements of Archaeology* published in 1822, 1823, and 1825.

At the same time as the Mechanics' Institutes and the *Encyclopaedias* were being born, the upper middle classes were being instructed in geology and archaeology by the *Spectator*, the *Gentleman's Magazine*, and the *Athenaeum*. John Mitford became editor of the *Gentleman's Magazine* in 1824 and filled it with antiquarian and archaeological information and discussion. It was thought to be quite natural in the middle of the nineteenth century that a man interested in antiquarian pursuits should subscribe to the Society of Antiquaries and to the *Gentleman's Magazine*. The *Magazine* itself published articles with a clear idea of why and what antiquarianism was: in the issue for 1829 we read:

> It is not the business of an Antiquary merely to decipher, transcribe and to pile document upon document, extract upon extract. . . . The judicious Antiquary has higher views than these: it is . . . to draw strong conclusions out of minute facts which have escaped the general eye . . . without the exertion of a conjectural spirit, guided by sober caution, the Antiquary would indeed be little better than a heaper up of old bills, inventories, ballads, a dealer in verdigris and iron rust, or a collector of . . . bricks, stones, tiles and pipkins . . .

Especially notable in the *Gentleman's Magazine* were the Antiquarian Notes edited for it by Charles Roach Smith.

In 1846 W. J. Thoms began a series of articles in the *Athenaeum* under the pseudonym of Ambrose Merton. These articles, to which he gave the title 'Folklore', dealt with all kinds of antiquarian subjects; they were so popular and caused such a great deal of correspondence that Wentworth Dilke, then editor and part proprietor of the paper, suggested to Thoms that he should start a special journal to deal popularly with the study of antiquities. The result was *Notes and Queries*, the first number of which appeared in November 1849.

There was no doubt that the public were interested in prehistory and early man, whether their interest sprang from natural science and geology or from something which can only be described baldly as the 'romance of excavation'. Certainly the romantic story of excavations in the Near East was a very early compulsive interest for the public at large. And, when one looks back at the story of archaeological

discovery – what splendid and exciting things had happened –
Botta finding Nineveh, or thinking he had found it (he was
really digging at Khorsabad – Dur Sharrukin, Sargon II's
city), Layard finding the palace of Sennacherib at Kuyunjik
with its great library of cuneiform tablets, Rawlinson hanging
over the cliff face at Behistun taking paper squeezes of the
trilingual inscriptions engraved in 516 B.C. on the order of
Darius Hystaspes, or that great moment in 1855 when the
country boats and rafts which were carrying downstream all
the finds made by Oppert, Fresnel, and Thomas in south
Mesopotamia and the two hundred and forty cases of material
from Khorsabad and from Ashur-bani-pal's palace at Nineveh,
were maliciously capsized by Arab brigands at Kurnah, at the
head of the Shatt-el-Arab.

Austen Henry Layard began digging at Nimrud in 1845 and
he worked there from late in that year until mid 1847. Here
he discovered the palaces subsequently identified with the
Assyrian kings Ashur-nasir-pal, Essarhaddon, and Shalmaneser
III. It was from these excavations that the British Museum has
obtained some of its most priceless treasures – the huge winged
bulls, the sculptures of Ashur-nasir-pal, and the black Obelisk
of Shalmaneser III. In 1847 the *Morning Post* published dis-
patches from its correspondent who visited Layard's work at
Nimrud. Layard thought he had identified Nineveh in the
remains at Nimrud just as Botta thought he had done at
Khorsabad. When he returned to England he published a book
entitled *The Monuments of Nineveh*, but also a popular account
of his excavations, *Nineveh and its Remains*. This was in 1848
and 1849. This popular account – surely the earliest and one
of the most successful of archaeological best-sellers – was very
widely read. It became an instant success; in a letter Layard
mentioned that eight thousand copies were sold in one year,
'which', he added 'will place it side by side with Mrs Run-
dell's *Cookery*'. This book was published by John Murray who
had also published Dennis's *Cities and Cemeteries of Etruria* and

Fellows's *First and Second Excursions in Asia Minor*. A year or so later Murray's produced the first series of books for reading in the train: they were for sale in the new bookstalls which W. H. Smith had been opening. Among the first half-dozen titles was an abridgement of *Nineveh and its Remains*; the title was *A Popular Account of Discoveries at Nineveh*. Could there be any clearer proof that just over a hundred years ago the public was very much interested in prehistory and archaeology?

And in the next few decades other archaeological books were best-sellers. Lyell's *Antiquity of Man* – 'a trilogy on the antiquity of man, Ice and Darwin', as a reviewer called it in *The Saturday Review* – was first published in February 1863. A second edition was called for in the following April, and a third in the succeeding November. As William Pengelly declared, with joy, 'three editions of a bulky scientific work in less than a few months'. We have already referred to the publication in 1865 of *Prehistoric Times* by Lord Avebury (then John Lubbock); this too was published by John Murray, was a good seller, and went on selling for half a century and more.

Of course those were the days when the intellectual world seemed very intimately concerned in the findings of geology, archaeology, and biology. Darwin's *Origin of Species* came out in 1859, and it was in the following year that the exciting debate took place in the British Association meeting at Oxford when T. H. Huxley, 'Darwin's watchdog', as he once described himself, sparred with the Bishop of Oxford, Soapy Sam Wilberforce. Huxley had described the *Origin of Species* as 'a flash of light . . . on a dark night'. Bishop Wilberforce, a man who, to quote William Irvine's joint biography of Darwin and Huxley, 'was one of those men whose moral and intellectual fibres have been permanently loosened by the early success and applause of a distinguished undergraduate career',* turned to Huxley and 'begged to know, was it

* W. Irvine, *Apes, Angels and Victorians*, London, 1955, p. 6.

through his grandfather or his grandmother that he claimed his descent from a monkey' – the remark which made Huxley slap the astonished knee of the scientist next to him as he muttered, 'The Lord hath delivered him into mine hands', and to make the famous speech in which he said he would be 'ashamed to be connected with a man who used great gifts to obscure the truth'. And it was the following year and also at Oxford that Benjamin Disraeli said, 'What is the question now placed before society with a glib assurance the most astounding? The question is this – Is man an ape or an angel? My Lord, I am on the side of the angels.'

The early public interest in geology and archaeology was very closely mixed up with religion and with the discussion of preconceived religious notions. Archaeology and geology were popular for two directly opposed reasons: first they seemed dangerous to accepted thought, therefore notorious, therefore interesting and news; but, secondly, they might lead to a new philosophy of man, therefore famous, therefore also interesting and news. The result was the same from whatever point of view you started; geology and archaeology were interesting. 'In the 1840s,' said G. M. Young, 'the religious world was divided into those who did not know what the geologists were saying and those who did not mind.' By the 1860s it was divided into those who knew perfectly well what the geologists were saying and did mind, and those who also knew well and didn't mind. Many feared the undermining influence of geology and archaeology on the mind; Blomfield would not allow ladies to attend geological lectures at King's College, London.

I think that it was this uncertainty as to whether archaeology was respectable or not, whether it was going to undermine faith or support it, that was directly responsible for one of the great moments of popular interest in archaeology in the 1870s. The story of George Smith has often been told. He was a minor official in the Assyrian department of the British

Museum and had particularly interested himself in the transliteration of cuneiform. He published in 1871 *The History of Ashur-bani-pal translated from the Cuneiform Inscriptions*. The next year, while working on the broken clay tablets from the Nineveh Library, he discovered a tablet which contained the statement that the ship rested on the mountains of Nizur, followed by the account of the sending forth of the dove, and its finding no resting place and returning. 'I saw at once,' said George Smith, 'that I had discovered a portion at least of the Chaldean account of the Deluge.' He later discovered further fragments of the same tablet and fragments of a duplicate text. From all this he was able to piece together a very great deal of the Babylonian Flood story; and this account he read to the Society for Biblical Archaeology in December 1872. It must have been an exciting moment coming as it did only just over a decade since Darwin and Huxley had been saying, or had seemed to be saying, that the Bible was not true, that man was descended from an ape, and that geology and archaeology were disposing of some of the cherished fundamentals of Victorian religious belief.

Now, if one listened to George Smith, here was archaeology proving the truth of the Flood story; it was apparently most definitely on the side of the angels. No wonder that the interest in George Smith's discovery was enormous. A portion of the tablets recording the Deluge story was missing and the *Daily Telegraph* offered £1,000 to equip an expedition led by George Smith to look for the missing fragment. The fact that Smith himself had never been on an excavation before and indeed never been in the Near East does not concern us here; nor is it our concern except in passing to record that by an amazing stroke of beginner's luck he found the missing fragment on the fifth day of his excavations. What concerns us here is that the press and the public had this archaeological interest in the seventies. George Smith published general accounts of his work in his *Assyrian Discoveries* and his *The*

Chaldean Account of Genesis. This latter book, like Layard's *Nineveh*, became a best-seller.

I do not want to dwell any longer on these points of detail but only to insist that in the great formative period of archaeology – the thirty years from 1840 to 1870 – there was an enormous popular interest in the subject. This has continued to our time fanned by excitements like Schliemann's discovery of Troy and Mycenae, Arthur Evans's discovery of Minoan Crete, the discovery of the Sumerian and Indus civilizations, the realization that there had been a great Hittite civilization. Many of us can remember very clearly the thrill of first hearing of discoveries like that of Howard Carter and Lord Caernarvon at Tutankhamen's Tomb, Sir Leonard Woolley at Ur, or the discovery by four schoolboys of the Upper Palaeolithic painted and engraved cave of Lascaux. This interest has been fostered by various agencies of communication – the *Illustrated London News*, for example, which, since 1900 under the editorship of Sir Bruce Ingram, has given constantly a large amount of space to archaeology, and *Antiquity*, a journal founded in 1925 deliberately to bring together the interested public and professional archaeologists, and, in the last fifteen years, sound and television programmes of the B.B.C.

But it is a commonplace that to trace the evolution of a thing is not to explain or indeed understand it. Why has the public this interest in prehistory and archaeology? In the first place the answer is that there is a widespread interest in history, and an interest in prehistory is just an extension of this general interest. 'Man is an historical animal,' wrote Professor Geoffrey Barraclough recently, 'with a deep sense of his own past, and if he cannot integrate the past by a history explicit and true, he will integrate it by a history implicit and false.' * If you begin to exercise your interest in the past and want an authentic account of what happened in the past, there is no reason why your interest should stop with the Victorians or

* Geoffrey Barraclough, *History in the Changing World*, 1956, pp. 24–5.

the Tudors or the Carolingians or the Romans or the Ancient
Britons or the Egyptians, and should not extend right back
to the La Tène Celts, the megalith builders, the first Neolithic
farmers of Jericho and Hasunna and Jarmo, and the Upper
Palaeolithic artists of Lascaux and Altamira.

Many have argued that we cannot make the exercise of historical imagination required by prehistory and that once we
go back beyond writing the achievements and the peoples
who made these achievements seem remote and almost sub-
human. I do not think that this is right and I like to think that
a story told by Professor Fleure in the preface to the last volume of *The Corridors of Time* is encouraging and typical. It
is a story about his collaborator H. J. E. Peake who had
created a chronological series in the Newbury Museum designed to show how inadequate are our ordinary school history books with their few remarks on Caesar and the Gallic
War and the Anglo-Saxon invasion wiping out the native
population. A result of this was shown when a school inspec-
tor spoke of things that had happened 'very long ago', and a
Newbury child interrupted him and said, 'Oh, but that was
quite lately, in the La Tène period.'*

Apart from this general historical reason there are, it seems
to me, four special reasons why prehistory is especially interesting in itself to the general public. In the first place, and not to
put too fine a point upon it, origins are especially fascinating
and the first of everything has a most especial interest and
attraction. From our childhood we have always wanted to
know who first thought of this, who first invented that, and
when we have become older and faced with problems of be-
haviour, life, human relations, the relations of states, property,
religion we have liked to turn to questions of origins, and to
ask ourselves questions like 'When was war invented?' 'When
did man believe in gods?' 'Were the first human beings

* H. Peake and H. J. Fleure, *Times and Places*, p. iii, being Volume x of
The Corridors of Time, 1956.

promiscuous or was monogamy the rule?' 'Is slavery a very old institution?' 'Were there always kings and priests?' 'Was there a Golden Age from which modern man has fallen or have we advanced steadily from apes to Victorians, from hand axes to Harwell?' That prehistory cannot supply the answer to so many of these questions is beside the point; it is all the while closely concerned with origins, and allied to the interest in beginnings is the sense of the incredibly remote and ancient which comes from the study of prehistory. The first Pharaohs were five thousand years ago but the artists who painted on the walls of Niaux and Lascaux may have lived thirty thousand years ago, and the makers of Abbevillian hand axes may have lived five hundred thousand years ago. We shall talk later about relevance, but here, when we contemplate the long millennia during which prehistoric man flourished, we feel only too ready to think that the history of the last five thousand years – Egypt, Assyria, Greece, Rome, and the Western world of Modern History – is almost, from a long chronological point of view, insignificant. Origins, and the great remoteness and ancientness of prehistoric man certainly give a glamour, although, as we shall argue, probably a meretricious one, to prehistory.

In the second place prehistory is interesting to the ordinary man in the street because its sources are so much nearer to the average person and his life than are the sources on which the historian *sensu stricto* relies. The historian works on papers in the Public Record Office, in our national libraries, in college and cathedral muniment rooms, and in the strong-rooms of country houses, county archive offices, and in parish chests. The prehistorian works on material in museums, it is true, and it is also true that this material is often as remote (or more remote) from the general public as documents in record offices; but often, owing to the enlightened policies of museum curators and committees and to enlightened schemes of display, very accessible. The prehistorian also works on material which he finds by that painstaking surgery of the landscape which we call excavation. He works, also, on field monuments which are visible to all – stone circles, lynchets, barrows, megalithic tombs, hut circles, hill forts – these things, the cultural fossils of prehistory which are part of our present-day cultural landscape – the dead, non-functional part of the landscape. But, though dead and non-functional, they are, unlike the dead documents in a cathedral library, available always for us to see, constant reminders of prehistory as we go to work or drive on holiday. They are marked on our Ordnance Survey maps with an exemplary zeal and thoroughness in a fashion which is the envy of most European countries; there are even special maps of *Ancient Britain* so that these prehistoric sites should not escape us and so that they should indeed become the objects of our holiday planning. And if we are bored with them there are always our children who want to see Stonehenge and Hadrian's Wall and who will not let their questions go unanswered when we drive them past Maiden Castle or Hetty Pegler's Tump and they say: 'What is that? How old? Why was it built, and by whom?'

Because of its strong surviving component in our landscape, prehistory is ever very much with us. I sometimes wonder whether the differential survival of field monuments in different countries has not had something to do with the differential development of public interest in prehistory in those countries. In France, for example, where in the vineyard-crowded areas of Languedoc and Gascony few field monuments survive, or where in the intensely cultivated Île de France most things have been ploughed away, it is not surprising that in those areas interest in prehistory is as little as it is great in the southern Morbihan, where almost every walk must bring one to a megalithic tomb. But I digress: my point here is a very simple one. A drive from Marlborough to Devizes passes barrows, Silbury Hill, Avebury, Wansdyke. In the face of these constant challenges in the surrounding landscape it

would indeed be a strange man who did not, however grudg-
ingly, ask some questions and demand some answers, even if
at first he was satisfied with simple answers like Druids and
Ancient Britons and at last he turned to Atlantis and Old
Straight Tracks.

But it is not only the sources of prehistoric archaeology
that appeal to the general public. Its methods are also of great
interest; the immediacy and accessibility of the sources are
equalled in general interest by the uniqueness and fascination
of archaeological method and technique. Air photography,
excavation, Carbon-14 analysis, the delicate operation of
piecing together broken pottery, and the restoration of a
corroded and decayed metal object, the study of bodies found
in peat bogs, the fact that we can obtain historical data by
analysing the contents of a prehistoric stomach – all these and
many other things have a special fascination by the very remoteness and intriguing nature of the techniques themselves.
Archaeological research has a great deal of the nature of detective work in it; indeed, so, of course, has all research, but it is
not often, as in archaeology, that the non-specialist can follow
all the stages and understand all the moves in this game of research and detection. The great researches in the natural and
physical sciences are also full of excitement, but they are
often much harder to follow and involve a knowledge of complicated processes and unfamiliar laboratory techniques which
the ordinary reader does not possess and cannot easily secure.
And, of course, these techniques and methods used by the
archaeologist are, in the most strict sense of the word, scientific. Here perhaps, as Angus Wilson has pointed out, lies one
of the satisfactions which prehistoric archaeology offers: 'A
humane study that increasingly calls upon scientific techniques,' he wrote, 'offers, in however limited a sphere, a reso-
lution of the ominous dichotomy between man's two intellectual approaches.'*

* *Observer*, 30 September 1956.

I have already referred to the romance of archaeology and to how the ordinary member of the public warms to the stories of adventure, of luck, and of chance in which the chronicle of archaeology abounds. Every undergraduate, if not every schoolboy, knows how the great painted cave of Lascaux in the Dordogne was discovered by chance by four schoolboys out rabbiting in September 1940 in the lightly wooded hills near the village of Montignac-sur-Vézère (now Montignac-Lascaux, such is the fame of prehistory). The fine gold ornament usually known as the Grunty Fen torc – it is made of a square-section bar of gold grooved to form four leaves, and then twisted, and is four feet in length – was found by accident by a peat-digger working in the fen near Cambridge. Stories like the finding of Lascaux and the finding of the Grunty Fen torc are legion; indeed it might be said with justice that a very great number of archaeological finds are made by chance. This aspect of chance discovery, the fact that on holiday or when digging in one's garden or excavating sewer trenches one may come across something which is of archaeological interest keeps the ordinary person near to archaeology and warms him to prehistory in a way which I do not think he can be warmed towards history constructed from written sources. After all it is extremely unlikely that one may find a valuable manuscript while digging in one's back garden, but it is quite possible that one may find a hand axe or a palstave.

There are, then, four reasons, as I see it, why prehistory at present is popular and appeals to people even more than ordinary history does – its remoteness and its concern with origins, its immediacy as a challenging part of our landscape, the fascination of its archaeological methods and techniques, and the romance and chance of discovery. But these are surely only reasons for intensifying an interest in prehistory. The basic interest in prehistory, as in history, is because we want to know what happened in the past and because we want re-created for us the historical contexts of prehistory.

But is finding out what happened in the past sufficient reason for a study of prehistory as of history, sufficient reason for the maintenance of teachers and researchers into prehistory, as into history? Are prehistorians then no more than chroniclers, or do they study the past as some explanation of the present and some guide to the future? This is an issue that has been debated a very great deal by historians in the strict sense of scholars whose main sources are literary and epigraphical. Professor T. F. Tout, for example, had no doubt that chronicle was the aim: 'We investigate the past,' he wrote, 'not to deduce practical political lessons but to find out what really happened.'* Others have been equally forceful on the other side: 'We seek the end to know "what really happened",' says Professor Geoffrey Barraclough, 'in order to assess its bearing and meaning for us. For it is simply not true that the past (as is so often stated) exists for itself.'† I must say at once that I am in agreement with Barraclough; we do not all the time study the past for itself, not even the remote prehistoric past can be studied in complete detachment. We must study it with an eye on its relevance to ourselves at the present day.

Now I know that here we enter on very debatable ground. There are those who say that prehistory is so far away from us that it can have no relevance at all to the present, that the red deer hunters of Seamer, the flint-miners of Spiennes, and the metal-workers of Hallstatt have nothing to tell us who live so many centuries later and in such a different state of material economy and culture. This is a position maintained by some who are prepared to admit that modern history is relevant to the present – even using modern history in the widest sense of everything that happened since the fall of Constantinople. Scholars have argued that prehistory is so limited by its methods and its absence of literary sources – its

* T. F. Tout, *Chapters in the Administrative History of Mediaeval England*, 1, 1920, p. 7.
† G. Barraclough, *History in a Changing World*, p. 23.

reliance on the surviving remains of the past – that it can have little relevance to us anyway; it is argued that its judgements must be so subjective. To quote Barraclough again: 'The history we read though based on facts is, strictly speaking, not factual at all, but a series of accepted judgements.'* If this is so for history proper how much more is it so for prehistory or history improper as it is sometimes cynically called. In prehistory, as we have seen in these lectures, we are always moving from one set of judgements to another, and what is a fact turns out to be what is currently accepted. In all this is there any historical certainty, and do prehistorians really know what is going on in the past? If they really are unsure of what happened in the prehistoric past, what is the point of arguing the relevance of what is uncertain, and anyway, so long ago, to the present?

That is how one groups speaks and they can argue a case. Another group of people thinks it unwise and even improper to think about the relevance of prehistory to the present. It is the same group of people which does not want prehistory popularized or vulgarized – but here the issue is one of interpretation not popularization. The same problem faces the historian all the time. It is often said that he should not interpret, should not assess the relevance of what he thinks happened in the past. But he is the person best qualified to do so, and if he does not, then the amateurs and publicists and propagandists will be left in possession of the field. 'If the accurate, judicious, and highly trained fail to draw the lessons of history,' writes C. V. Wedgwood, 'the unscrupulous and unqualified will do it for them.'† It must surely be one of the main tasks of the prehistorian to interpret and to assess the contemporary relevance of the facts which the archaeological researches of his colleagues and himself produce. This is, in my view, one of the main spheres in which the idea of

* G. Barraclough, *History in a Changing World*, p. 14.
† C. V. Wedgwood, *Velvet Studies*, 1946, p. 156.

prehistory has not yet fulfilled itself. It cannot be pretended that there is anything approaching a philosophy of prehistory; yet it is precisely in this sphere of the philosophical relevance of prehistory to ourselves that prehistory may have most to contribute to the public.

Let us consider very briefly some of these underlying relevancies, and I say very briefly because it has been my concern in these lectures not to give you my idea of the perspective of prehistory but to discuss with you how the idea of prehistory has developed and changed. I think the first and most overwhelming relevancy is the universality of time and space in early human history. For so long we have thought in the Western world that we were the heirs of the Greek and Roman civilizations as they were of the civilizations of Crete, Mesopotamia, and Egypt; now we see, quite apart from the historians who are insisting very rightly that eastern Europe and Russia are as much the heirs of the classical civilization of the Mediterranean as the West, and that any evaluation of European civilization which forgets the contribution of the Arabs forgets a great deal, that Greece and Rome, Assyria, Babylon, and Egypt are only some elements in the long and complicated story of the development of man from the Palaeolithic 'savagery' that produced Altamira and Lascaux to the present day. The cities of Mohenjo-Daro and Harappa in Pakistan, of Anyang in China, of Chichen Itza and Palenque in Central America are as relevant to our overall picture of the human past as are Ur and Athens. Whether we be Americans, Russians, Indians, or Chinese we share a universal human historical heritage. I do not pretend, or imagine, that a recognition of this fact will alter present-day differences but if people really had an awareness of human history it should put present-day differences in a different perspective and one that made for tolerance.

It is the length of the perspective of prehistory which more than any one thing is to me the contribution of prehistory to modern thought. Let us recollect its essentials. Man, as a sentient upright-walking, talking, tool-making animal came into existence some three quarters to two thirds of a million years ago. After millennia of brutish life with little surviving material equipment, and a spiritual and moral equipment at which we can only guess, we find him at the end of the Ice Age not only a superb craftsman in flintwork – as witness, for example, Solutrean laurel leaves – but an artist, making beautiful spear-throwers, sculpturing horses and human beings on the walls of his rock-shelter houses and penetrating into the dark depths of deep caves to establish there cult-shrines, where in front of engravings and paintings and even models of animals, magico-religious rites were carried out. And all this art was at least fifteen thousand years ago and possibly as early as thirty thousand years. Somewhere, perhaps at ten thousand years B.C., we find man in some localities in the Near East discovering how to cultivate wheat and barley: agriculture has begun – a discovery that may have been made independently in India and South China and as we know now appears certainly to have been made independently in America. At the same time or later, in the same area of the Near East or in neighbouring areas, animals were domesticated, and from these twin bases of cultivation and domestication the peasant village communities of the Old and New Worlds came into existence. From the single basis of domestication came into existence the nomad societies of Arabia, North Africa, and Central Asia.

Very gradually as we look into the record of prehistory we see the settled peasant village communities in the Near East, in India and China and in Central America develop and prosper so that large communities appear which are towns or cities and which have complex trade relationships and a specialization of labour, which can communicate by writing, and have priests and kings or chiefs; to these organizations we must be prepared, in any objective terminology, to give the name civilization.

What is perhaps most dramatic as we reflect on this long process is the length of time which the earlier stages have taken. No one suggests that the so-called Neolithic revolution – the change to a food-producing economy based on cultivation and domestication – started anywhere in the world before ten to twelve thousand years ago, and until recently this date would have been given as nearer six to seven thousand years ago. Yet man himself – man by definition as *homo sapiens* – was in existence six hundred thousand years ago. We as food producers with a life built on villages and cities have only been in existence for one sixtieth of man's time on earth. Do these figures of thousands of years mean anything to you? Think of the face of a clock, and of a minute hand going round for an hour. Fifty-nine minutes of that hour represents man the food-gatherer, man in the stage of Palaeolithic savagery, man in the Old Stone Age. In the last minute but one we see him painting at Lascaux and Altamira and Niaux, but it is only at the beginning of the last minute that we see him gaining control over the cultivation of grain and the domestication of animals – it is only then that the Neolithic Revolution takes place, and only in the last half-minute that the social, material, and cultural changes we call civilization occur. Egypt, Sumeria, Greece, Rome, Christianity, Buddhism, the pre-Columbian civilizations of America – all these have occurred in that last half-minute of man's long life on earth. This does not mean that they are irrelevant; but it does mean, at least to me, that their relative importance is less. You remember the philosophy which George Borrow put into a sentence in *Lavengro*: 'There's night and day . . . sun, moon and stars . . . likewise a wind on the heath, brother.' True, but to me it is a wind that blows from ancient, dimly apprehended, prehistoric heaths, and that tells us that man is very old, and that the present with its ideological conflicts, its threats of destruction by nuclear warfare on the one hand and by overpopulation on the other, is not necessarily the end of existence, an existence that is already sixty times as long as the beginnings of agriculture and nearly a hundred times as long as the inventions of writing and formalized religions. I think there is a relevance to present thought in our knowledge of prehistory even if the philosophical elements of it are only roughly and crudely thought out as yet.

In his *Modern Historians and the Study of History*, a book of essays published in 1955, Professor F. M. Powicke says:

The function of history is not to trace back the institutions and ways of thought which have survived as though we were at the end and climax of history. It is at least as important to retrieve the treasures that have been dropped on the way and lost, which if restored would enrich our civilization.

Here I think is the final and real justification of prehistory, its relevance to us, and the reason why it has a popular interest. The real justification is not in origins, or techniques, or in perspective, but in pleasure; the pleasure of prehistory is in the recovery of the treasures of man's prehistoric past that have been dropped on the way and lost. Whatever is missing from the record of the prehistoric past much survives of its achievement in the visual arts, and we can today admire and enjoy the beauty, for example, of the leaping cows at Lascaux, the brilliant simplicity and purity of line of the stylized Cycladic figurines (Plate 8), the assured craftsmanship of the owls and bulls of the Brå cauldron, the architectural mastery of the builders of Stonehenge. We may find Upper Palaeolithic art or the art of the early Jerichoans who moulded features in clay on to human skulls, very remote in time, but they are not remote in spirit or aesthetic understanding, achievement, or inspiration. It is the transcendental character of the visual arts that emerges so clearly and perhaps unexpectedly from the study of prehistory. We may not be able to think ourselves back into the rock-shelters of Upper Palaeolithic man or, perhaps fortunately, into the filth and stench that must have existed in the houses at Skara Brae and Little Woodbury, but the artistic achievements of prehistory require no effort of the imagination in their appreciation. The art of prehistoric man is part of the universal heritage of mankind, and it is sad that as yet it occupies only a small part in the formal histories of art. These usually begin with a few reproductions of Upper Palaeolithic art and then turn hastily to the art of the Egyptian and Sumerian civilizations. Admittedly, for a fuller understanding of prehistoric art, we need to know something of the chronological structure of prehistory and the culture of the varying societies that produced the art; we should have an idea of prehistory if we are to see prehistoric art in its chronological and cultural perspective. But even without that we can enjoy the artistic creations of prehistoric man. The treasures of prehistory do enrich our own civilization, and it is the excitement of the discovery and study and appreciation of the enrichment which is to me the main component of the idea of prehistory which we have at the present day.

BOOKS FOR FURTHER READING

*

INDEX

BOOKS FOR FURTHER READING

No authoritative and definitive history of archaeology and prehistory has as yet been published. A. Michaelis, *A Century of Archaeological Discoveries* (London, 1908) dealt with discovery, mainly in classical lands, up to the beginning of the nineteenth century. This was a translation of his *Die archäologischen Entdeckungen des neunzehnten Jahrhunderts* (Leipzig, 1906), and Friedrich von Oppeln-Bronikowski's *Die archäologischen Entdeckungen im 20 Jahrhundert* (Berlin, 1931) takes the story on another thirty years. My own *Hundred Years of Archaeology* (London, 1950) dealt in summary form mainly with the development of prehistoric archaeology in the period 1840–1940. For more popular accounts of the history of archaeology see W. H. Boulton, *The Romance of Archaeology* (London, n.d.), C. W. Ceram, *Gods, Graves and Scholars* (London, 1952), and *A Picture History of Archaeology* (London, 1958). I do not repeat here the bibliographical details given in my *Hundred Years of Archaeology*, but special mention must be made of H. J. E. Peake, *The Study of Prehistoric Times* (Huxley Memorial Lecture for 1940), *J. R. Anthrop. Inst.*, 1940, 1.

The story of Mesopotamian archaeology is well told in Seton Lloyd's *Foundations in the Dust* (London, 1947); see also E. A. W. Budge, *The Rise and Progress of Assyriology* (London, 1925); and of Aegean archaeology in Sir John Myres, *The Cretan Labyrinth* (Huxley Memorial Lecture for 1933), *J. R. Anthrop. Inst.*, 1933, p. 269. The general story of archaeology through the discovery of lost cities can be read in Marcel Brion's *La Résurrection des Villes Mortes* (Paris, 1948), and more popularly in Hermann and Georg Schreiber, *Vanished Cities* (London, 1958) and Leonard Cottrell's *Lost Cities* (London, 1957).

Geoffrey Bibby's *The Testimony of the Spade* (London, 1957) deals with the development of European prehistory, and is especially good on Northern archaeology; Colin Simard's *Découverte archéologique de la France* (Paris, 1955) deals mainly with the story of French Palaeolithic discovery, as does the Abbé Breuil's *The Discovery of the Antiquity of Man: Some of the Evidence* (being the Huxley Memorial

Lecture for 1941, delivered in 1946), *J. R. Anthrop. Inst.*, 1945, p. 21. A fuller account of the development of French archaeology is in R. Lantier, 'Un Siècle d'archéologie protohistorique' in *Congrès archéologique de France*, 1935. The development of German archaeology is well described in J. H. Eggers, *Einführung in die Vorgeschichte* (Munich, 1959).

For British archaeology see Sir Thomas Kendrick's *The Druids* (London, 1927), *British Antiquity* (London, 1950), and 'The British Museum and British Antiquities', in *Antiquity*, 1954, p. 132; H. B. Walters, *The English Antiquaries of the 16th, 17th and 18th centuries* (London, 1934) and Stuart Piggott's *William Stukeley* (Oxford, 1950), and the following articles and lectures: 'Prehistory and the Romantic Movement', *Antiquity*, 1937, p. 31; 'The Sources of Geoffrey of Monmouth', *Antiquity*, 1941, pp. 269 and 305; 'Stukeley, Avebury and the Druids', *Antiquity*, 1935, p. 22; 'The Ancestors of Jonathan Oldbuck', *Antiquity*, 1955, p. 150; 'William Camden and the *Britannia*' (Reckitt Archaeological Lecture for 1951), *Proc. Brit. Acad.*, XXXVII, p. 199; 'Antiquarian Thought in the Sixteenth and Seventeenth Centuries' in (Ed. Levi Fox) *English Historical Scholarship in the Sixteenth and Seventeenth Centuries* (London, O.U.P. for the Dugdale Society, 1956). Valuable for the topographical aspects of the early antiquaries is E. G. R. Taylor, *Tudor Geography* (London, 1930), and *Late Tudor and Stuart Geography* (London). Dr Joan Evans's *A History of the Society of Antiquaries of London* (London, 1956) and her *Time and Chance* (London, 1943) are mirrors of British archaeology seen from the standpoint of one Society and one family. Also may be consulted E. Moir, 'The English Antiquaries', *History Today*, 1958, p. 781 and G. E. Daniel, 'Who were the Welsh?' (Rhŷs Memorial Lecture for 1954), *Proc. Brit. Acad.*, XL, p. 145.

Stanley Casson, *The Discovery of Man* (London, 1939) is a general survey of the development of archaeology and anthropology. For the history of anthropology see A. C. Haddon and A. H. Quiggin, *History of Anthropology* (London, 1934), T. K. Penniman's *A Hundred Years of Anthropology* (second ed., London, 1952), and R. H. Lowie, *The History of Ethnological Theory* (London, 1937). A more popular survey is to be found in H. R. Hayes, *From Ape to Angel* (London, 1959).

For the history of geology see Sir Archibald Geikie, *Founders of*

Geology (second ed., London, 1905), A. C. Ramsay, *Passages in the History of Geology* (London, 1848 and 1849), H. B. Woodward, *History of Geology* (London, n.d.) and *History of the Geological Society of London* (London, 1907).

The impact of scientific discoveries upon religious beliefs in the decades before Darwin is well told in C. C. Gillispie's *Genesis and Geology* (Volume LVIII of the *Harvard Historical Studies*, 1951, reprinted as a Harper Torchbook, New York, 1959), with an excellent bibliography. Invaluable here also is A. D. White, *A History of the Warfare of Science with Theology in Christendom* (1896). For books about individual geologists see T. G. Bonney, *Charles Lyell and Modern Geology* (London, 1901), Mrs Gordon's *Life of William Buckland* (London, 1894), Katherine M. Lyell's *Life, Letters and Journals of Sir Charles Lyell* (London, 1881), P. Chalmers Mitchell, *Thomas Henry Huxley* (London, 1913), A. Ledieu, *Boucher de Perthes* (Paris 1885), and L. Aufrère, *Essai sur les premières découvertes de Boucher de Perthes et les origines de l'archéologie primitive (1838–1844)*, Paris, 1936.

For special subjects A. O. Lovejoy's *The Great Chain of Being* (Harvard, 1942) and some of the essays in *Ideas and Beliefs of the Victorians* (foreword H. Grisewood, London, 1949) are germane to the discussion. The idea of progress itself was studied by J. B. Bury in his *The Idea of Progress* (1920). See also this same author's *Darwin and Modern Science* (London, 1909).

On Elliot Smith see (Ed. Warren R. Dawson) *Sir Grafton Elliot Smith: A Biographical Record by his Colleagues* (London, 1938) and Chapter X of Lowie's *History of Ethnological Theory*. Among recent works on Darwinism and Evolution and the Centenary of the antiquity of man see Loren Eiseley, *Darwin's Century* (London, 1959), William Irvine, *Apes, Angels and Victorians* (London, 1955) and (Ed. S. A. Barnett) *A Century of Darwin* (London, 1958). Also of interest here J. W. Judd, *The Coming of Evolution* (Cambridge, 1910), and Francis C. Haber, *The Age of the World: Moses to Darwin* (Baltimore, 1959).

For the work of individual archaeologists see Sir Leonard Woolley, *Spadework* (London, 1953), O. G. S. Crawford, *Said and Done* (London, 1955), Sir Mortimer Wheeler, *Still Digging* (London, 1955), and Ronald Clark, *Sir Mortimer Wheeler* (London, 1960); E. A. Wallis Budge, *By Nile and Tigris* (London, 1920), Sir Flinders Petrie,

Seventy Years of Archaeology (London, 1931), Emil Ludwig, *Schliemann: the Story of a Goldseeker* (London, 1931), Robert Payne, *Troy* (London, 1959), J. Beddoe, *Memories of Eighty Years* (London, 1910), C. Breasted, *Pioneer to the Past: the Story of J. H. Breasted, Archaeologist* (London, 1948), Sir E. Harrison, *Harrison of Ightham* (London, 1928), A. H. Layard, *Autobiography and Letters* (London, 1903), L. S. B. Leakey, *White African* (London, 1937), H. Pengelly, *A Memoir of William Pengelly* (London, 1897).

On the modern methods and techniques of archaeology and for an analysis of the methodology of prehistory consult Sir Mortimer Wheeler, *Archaeology from the Earth* (Oxford, 1954), O. G. S. Crawford, *Man and His Past* (London, 1921), V. Gordon Childe, *A Short Introduction to Archaeology* (London, 1956), and *Piecing together the Past* (London, 1956), J. G. D. Clark, *Archaeology and Society* (London, 1957, third ed.), Stuart Piggott, *Approach to Archaeology* (London, 1959), Sigfried De Laet, *Archaeology and its Problems* (London, 1957), R. J. C. Atkinson, *Field Archaeology* (London, 1954, second ed.), O. G. S. Crawford, *Archaeology in the Field* (London, 1953), Fr. Behn, *Vor-und Frühgeschichte* (Wiesbaden, 1948), P. de Palol, *Arqueología: Propósitos y Métodos* (Valladolid, 1958), G. R. Willey and P. Phillips, *Method and Theory in American Archaeology* (Chicago, 1958), W. W. Taylor, *A Study of Archaeology* (American Anth. Ass., Mem. 69, Menasha, 1948). For a special treatment of certain problems see V. Gordon Childe, *Social Evolution* (London, 1951) and for an attempt to set prehistory into a general historical perspective see Pierre Teilhard de Chardin, *The Phenomenon of Man* (London, 1959).

INDEX

MORE ABOUT PENGUINS
AND PELICANS

Penguinews, which appears every month, contains details of all the new books issued by Penguins as they are published. Fom time to time it is supplemented by *Penguins in Print*, which is a complete list of all available books published by Penguins. (There are well over three thousand of these.)

A specimen copy of *Penguinews* will be sent to you free on request, and you can become a subscriber for the price of the postage. For a year's issues (including the complete lists) please send 30p if you live in the United Kingdom, or 60p if you live elsewhere. Just write to Dept EP, Penguin Books Ltd, Harmondsworth, Middlesex, enclosing a cheque or postal order, and your name will be added to the mailing list.

Note: *Penguinews* and *Penguins in Print* are not available in the U.S.A. or Canada

LIAM DE PAOR

ARCHAEOLOGY

An illustrated introduction

Archaeology still has its treasures and its treasure-hunters, but today's archaeologist is essentially a master detective. From fragments of pottery or bone he reconstructs the life of communities which vanished fifty or a hundred centuries ago; from traces in a patch of earth he recovers the form of objects whose substance has long since ceased to exist; every year new finds help him to fit together the jigsaw of prehistory and to go further and further back into the human past.

The illustrations in this introduction to archaeology have been closely incorporated with the text. Dr Liam de Paor, himself a well-known archaeologist, shows how the study developed from eccentric amateur beginnings to its present-day scientific status. He describes its modern techniques – from air photography and varve analysis to Carbon 14 dating – its co-operation with other disciplines, and some of its unique and astonishing discoveries both in prehistory and in later periods.

NORA CHADWICK

THE CELTS

The Celtic character and imagination are still a vital part of our heritage and whilst the purest strain is probably in Ireland, in Scotland and Wales too their influence is unmistakable.

The Celts began to grow powerful and to spread across Europe from about 1200 B.C. They were, and are, taller and fairer than the Mediterranean people. They used chariots and were fond of display, achieving superb workmanship in drinking vessels, weapons and jewellery. They started landing in Britain in about the eighth century B.C. and in the East they spread as far as Asia Minor.

In this book Nora Chadwick, a Celtic scholar of international repute, describes the rise and spread of the Celts and their arrival in the British Isles, and includes an appreciation of their religion, art and literature in these islands. *The Celts* is a study of the people whose extraordinary individualistic and imaginative qualities have contributed so much to the world we live in today.

DONALD HARDEN

THE PHOENICIANS

Second to none as explorers and traders, the Phoenicians dominated the seas in the first millenium B.C. From a precarious foothold on the Levant coast they spread across the Mediterranean to establish a chain of colonies, the most important of which was Carthage. They carried raw materials and manufactured goods at least as far north as Brittany, and voyaged right round the continent of Africa.

This study introduces an influential but little known civilization, whose major contribution to the modern world was the development of the alphabet. Dr Harden, lifelong student of the Phoenicians, has assembled all the archaeological and literary evidence to outline their history, way of life and artistic achievements and to show how these were influenced by close contact with so many different cultures.

GLYN DANIEL

THE FIRST CIVILIZATIONS*

The Archaeology of their Origins

The first civilizations may be said to have come into being in Mesopotamia, Egypt, the Indus Valley and China in the old World; in Mexico, Yucatan and Peru in the New World.

Dr Glyn Daniel here examines the problem of the origins of these civilizations. Did they all develop from one centre and the process of civilization take place once, and once only, in human history, or did it occur independently in different parts of the world?

This and other related questions are discussed by Dr Daniel with style and perception in a completely new and fruitful way that makes entertaining and instructive reading.

THE ORIGINS AND GROWTH
OF ARCHAEOLOGY

In about three centuries archaeology has evolved from treasure-hunting and the quaint speculation of antiquarians into a meticulous discipline, absorbing techniques from other sciences in order to extract the maximum information from the slightest evidence. In this anthology of key writings Dr Glyn Daniel illustrates vividly the dramatic development of his subject. The early blunderings are illustrated by the extraordinary exploits of Belzoni, the romance of the heyday of discovery by Schliemann, Evans and Howard Carter. Later chapters document the equally exciting development of systematic excavation and of techniques for precise dating that would once have seemed impossible.

* Not for sale in the U.S.A.